ISSUES
IN
MISSIOLOGY

VOLUME I

PART 1A: PERSECUTION

ROBERT D. PATTON, M.D., D.D.

DISCLAIMER

The author of this work has quoted the writers of many articles and books. This does not mean that the author endorses or recommends the works of others. If the author quotes someone, it does not mean that he agrees with all of the author's tenets, statements, concepts, or words, whether in the work quoted or any other work of the author. There has been no attempt to alter the meaning of the quotes; and therefore, some of the quotes are long in order to give the entire sense of the passage.

Issues in Missiology, Vol. 1A: Persecution

(Previously, Volume 1 was 2 parts: Part A, persecution and Part B, money and partnerships. Dr. Patton has split Volume I into the 2 parts. 1A Persecution and 1B Money Matters)
Copyright © 2022 by Robert D. Patton, M.D., D.D.
Email: bobpatton@sr.net

All Rights Reserved
Printed in the United States of America

ISBN 978-1-7376384-7-6

BAPTIST WORLD MISSION
P.O. Box 2149
Decatur, Alabama 35602-2149
Telephone Number: 256-353-2221
Fax Number: 256-353-2266
E-mail: office@baptistworldmission.org

All Scripture quotes are from the King James Bible except those verses compared and then the source is identified.

Publishing and Formatting by:
THE OLD PATHS PUBLICATIONS, Inc.
142 Gold Flume Way
Cleveland, Georgia, U.S.A. 30528
Web: www.theoldpathspublications.com
E-mail: TOP@theoldpathspublications.com
1.0

DEDICATION

Dedicated to my beloved wife of over 62 years, M. Elizabeth Patton, faithful helpmeet, extraordinary soulwinner and discipler of women, co-worker in the ministry, mother of four children, grandmother of 18 grandchildren, and 16 great-grandchildren. Proverbs 31: [28] *Her children arise up, and call her blessed; her husband also, and he praiseth her.*

FOREWORD

Dr. Robert Patton, veteran missionary with Baptist World Mission, has spent 34 years overseas. As a small boy, he accompanied his parents for 38 months in a prisoner-of-war camp in the Philippine Islands during World War II. From 1971-1976, he was Professor of Internal Medicine developing a program of Internal Medicine in a new medical school in Monrovia, Liberia. And from 1986-2012, he spent 26 years in Suriname, South America, primarily in church planting, Bible translation, development of discipleship materials, developing two Bible Institutes, and broadcasting over radio and television.

Dr. Patton has been burdened for three groups: those who have never heard; those who are untaught, and those who are being persecuted. Those who have not heard are unreached with the gospel; those who are untaught need the Word of God in their own mother tongue; and those who suffer persecution are located primarily in Muslim or communist countries.

In Volume I of Issues in Missiology, Dr. Patton addresses two challenges: Persecution, and Missions and Money. Christians are suffering in the third wave of persecution in the history of the church. The missionary needs to understand the nature and cause of persecution, and the proper Christian response. The missionary must also understand the dynamics of giving and the biblical principles involved, especially with the increasing discrepancy between financial resources in the west and in many parts of the developing.

A second volume in preparation will address two additional issues: Spiritual Warfare and Translation Issues.

The Pattons have four children 18 grandchildren, and 16 great-grandchildren. Dr. Patton and his wife Elizabeth relocated at Crown College in Powell, Tennessee, with a goal of impacting the next generation of missionaries.

TABLE OF CONTENTS

PERSECUTION

Introduction

The Bible is a book written by persecuted Christians for persecuted Christians during a time of great persecution. It is estimated that as many as 5 million Christians died in the first century after Christ. Today, the estimate is that more than 80% of all martyrs of the faith are Christian. One reported figure was 166,000 martyrs killed for the faith in 2003, and by the current date, it is estimated that the number will perhaps exceed 200,000.[1] Approximately 200,000,000 Christians are under threat of death, imprisonment, or torture, and an additional 400,000 suffer some sort of discrimination. [2]

Dietrich Bonhoeffer:
Martyr for Christ on the Grace of Suffering

Dietrich Bonhoeffer, a martyr for Christ killed by the Nazis during World War II, wrote the following: "Discipleship means allegiance to the suffering Christ, and it is therefore not at all surprising that Christians should be called upon to suffer."[3] Thus the Bible, especially the New Testament, was written **by** persecuted believers **for** persecuted believers and dealt especially with persecution for righteousness' sake.

In his book, *The Cost of Discipleship*, Bonhoeffer says: "When Christ calls a man, He calls him to die." Bonhoeffer was greatly concerned about "cheap grace," which is grace with no cost to the individual. By the phrase cheap grace, Bonhoeffer means the grace which has brought chaos and destruction; it is the intellectual assent to a doctrine without a real transformation in the sinner's life. It is the justification of the sinner without the works that should accompany the new birth. Bonhoeffer says of cheap grace:

"[It] is the preaching of forgiveness without requiring repentance, baptism without church discipline, communion

11

without confession, absolution without personal confession. Cheap grace is grace without discipleship, grace without the cross, grace without Jesus Christ, living and incarnate."[4]

Real grace, in Bonhoeffer's estimation, is a grace that will cost a man his life. It is the grace made dear by the life of Christ that was sacrificed to purchase man's redemption. Cheap grace arose out of man's desire to be saved, but to do so without becoming a disciple. The doctrinal system of the church, with its lists of behavioral codes, becomes a substitute for the Living Christ, and this cheapens the demands of true discipleship. A set of rules replaces the dynamic indwelling Holy Spirit empowering the disciple. The true believer must resist cheap grace and enter the life of active discipleship. Faith can no longer mean sitting still and waiting; the Christian must rise and follow Christ.

It is here that Bonhoeffer makes one of his most enduring claims on the life of the true Christian. He writes that "only he who believes is obedient, and only he who is obedient believes." Men have become soft and complacent in cheap grace and are thus cut off from the discovery of the more costly grace of self-sacrifice and personal debasement. Bonhoeffer believed that the teaching of cheap grace was the ruin of more Christians than any commandment of works.[5]

As we think about Bonhoeffer's contrast of cheap grace with costly grace, we begin to understand the whole area of persecution a bit more clearly. The persecuted Christian is unlikely to go along with cheap grace. He will either capitulate to his persecutors, or he will develop as a disciple. And through this process, the church is purified and God is glorified. God's grace is magnified.

Jozef Ton: Persecuted Romanian Theologian

Jozef Ton, who was beaten and imprisoned in Romania, has developed a very important theology of suffering and martyrdom. He points out that God's ultimate goal is to populate the universe with true believers who will share in the responsibilities of ruling the universe, who reflect the Lord Jesus Christ, and who bring glory to God Himself. He points out that our rewards in heaven have to do with reigning with Christ. We are placed here on earth where our character is developed and tested to prepare us for our future responsibilities. The trials and tribulations of this world both form our character and test our priorities to see how much responsibility we can handle in the future. God provides us with all we need, but we are responsible to allow Him to work in our lives. It appears that persecution does more than just test the individual's capabilities and commitment to the Lord, but that the development of his character is transmitted to his life after death as well as his life here on earth. This basic concept will be expanded later.[6]

Future Rewards and Suffering

The Bible has a number of terms concerning our future life in eternity with Him. These terms include the following: obtaining an inheritance, reigning with Christ, having treasures in heaven, or gaining rewards in heaven. We have a glorious future as believers, and He is working in our lives now to prepare us for this future. Unfortunately, often we focus on life on earth without thinking about a future eternal life in heaven.

God promises us incredible blessings in the future: *Revelation 1:[6] And hath made us kings and priests unto God and his Father; to him be glory and dominion for ever and ever. Amen. Revelation 5:[10] And hast made us unto our God kings and priests: and we shall reign on the earth.* Jozef Ton comments on these promises. To quote Ton: "He wants to make us kings like He is King but will only entrust such positions to them who obey Him as He obeyed His Father." Thus, God is working to make us resemble Jesus Christ.

The apostle Peter warns us as follows: *1 Peter 4:[12] Beloved, think it not strange concerning the fiery trial which is to try you, as the though some strange thing happened to you. [13] But rejoice, inasmuch as ye are partakers of Christ's sufferings;*

that, when his glory shall be revealed, ye shall be glad also with exceeding joy. Persecution purifies the church as well as the believers. We need cross-carrying messengers of a cross-centered gospel.

Jesus promised: *Acts 1:[8] But ye shall receive power, after that the Holy Ghost is come upon you: and ye shall be witnesses (martyrs) unto me both in Jerusalem, and all Judea, and in Samaria, and unto the uttermost part of the earth.* The Greek word, marturia, from which we derive the word martyr, means witness. Thus, Jesus says that you shall be martyrs.

We in the USA have suffered little persecution. It is very hard for us to imagine or identify with those who do. Persecution is not the equivalent of suffering. All people suffer at one time or another, but not all people suffer persecution. Persecution is suffering for righteousness' sake. *Mt. 5:[10] Blessed are they which are persecuted for righteousness' sake: for theirs is the kingdom of heaven. [11] Blessed are ye, when men shall revile you, and persecute you, and shall say all manner of evil against you falsely, for my sake.[12] Rejoice, and be exceeding glad: for great is your reward in heaven: for so persecuted they the prophets which were before you.*

Basic Biblical Concepts: Concepts in Creation

As we study the Bible in terms of persecution, the creation of man is extremely important. Man was created in the image of God, and thus has intrinsic worth, respect and dignity. *Genesis 1:[26] And God said, Let us make man in our image, after our likeness: and let them have dominion over the fish of the sea, and over the fowl of the air, and over the cattle, and over all the earth, and over every creeping thing that creepeth upon the earth.[27] So God created man in his own image, in the image of God created he him; male and female created He them. [28] And God blessed them, and God said unto them: Be fruitful, and multiply and replenish the earth, and subdue it and have dominion over the fish of the sea, and over the fowl of the air, and over every living thing that moveth upon the earth....[31] And God saw everything that He had made, and behold, it was very good. And the evening and the morning were the sixth day.* God works in creation even now on man's behalf.

God created man in His own image. Mankind could think, reason, have emotions and will. The very spirit of God could dwell in mankind. He was given dominion over the creation. God's goal was to have mankind fellowship with Him and rule over the entire created universe forever.

When man fell, and the image of God was marred, it was not eliminated. God still values the individual, even though he is now a sinner. *Genesis 9:[5] And surely your blood of your lives will I require; at the hand of every beast will I require it, and at the hand of man; at the hand of every man's brother will I require the life of man.[6] Whoso sheddeth man's blood, by man shall his blood be shed: for in the image of God made He man.* The basic responsibility to take a human life is now given to the government. The individual is not to take personal revenge, and man is still to be respected.

God's revealed character is found to be the basis of law. He expects us to act towards others as He acts towards us, because they are created in His image. God is concerned with minimal civil rights, especially to vulnerable groups such as widows, orphans, and strangers. These rights include the right to life, the right to be unharmed, the right to the necessities of life, and the right to protection of personal property. Humans have rights because God created them, protects them, and demands justice for them. God expects protection against such things as physical abuse, abortion, and being taken hostage.

When we do not respect man, we do not respect the God in whose image he is created! Islam and Communism do not acknowledge that man is created in the image of God. Islam specifically denies that any person can be like God and that God is entirely apart from all else in His creation (tawhid).

Communism denies the very existence of God. Therefore, neither belief has a philosophical basis for individual human rights, and neither group gives individuals these rights. Both groups are particularly virulent in their persecution of Christians. Their concept is that rights are given to a group, and not to individuals. They do not give intrinsic rights to humans because they do not accept that they are created in the image of God.

Furthermore, God is a Trinity and thus the God of relationships. Because we are created in the image of God, our rights also exist in the context of relationships. These rights include the right to worship in relationship with others. Our creation is also the basis for equality. Both men and women have rights. However, as the Trinity is not identical and likewise individuals are not identical.

In the framework of relationships between individuals who are different from each other, the three members of the godhead are bound together in love. True love is independent of the response of the individual who is loved. There must be freedom of the will to have true love. Thus, it must be possible for the created beings to reject or accept God in His position as creator. In his position as the image-bearer of God, man can reject God or obey and reverence Him. Satan will attack mankind precisely in this area of trust and obedience.

Basic Biblical Concepts: Satan and Persecution

God created both angels and mankind with free will. Freedom of will means that one is free to choose the wrong as well as the right. Free will allowed Lucifer to become Satan, the adversary. *Isaiah 14:[12] How art thou fallen from heaven, O Lucifer, son of the morning! how art thou cut down to the ground, which didst weaken the nations![13] For thou hast said in thine heart, I will ascend into heaven, I will exalt my throne above the stars of God: I will sit also upon the mount of the congregation, in the sides of the north:[14] I will ascend above the heights of the clouds; I will be like the most High.[15] Yet thou shalt be brought down to hell, to the sides of the pit.* It appears that Lucifer succeeded in convincing one third of the angels to follow him in rebellion. It also appears that once the angels made their choice, that choice became irreversible. Some churches like the universalist church believe that even demons can be saved. There is no evidence in scripture supporting this doctrine.

Satan now struggled with God for the loyalty of mankind. *Genesis 3:[1] Now the serpent was more subtil than any beast of the field which the LORD God had made. And he said unto the woman, Yea, hath God said, Ye shall not eat of every tree of the garden?[2] And the woman said unto the serpent, We may eat of the fruit of the trees of the garden:[3] But of the fruit of the tree which is in the midst of the garden, God hath said, Ye shall not eat of it, neither shall ye touch it, lest ye die.[4] And the serpent said unto the woman, Ye shall not surely die:[5] For God doth know that in the day ye eat thereof, then your eyes shall be opened, and ye shall be as gods, knowing good and evil.[6] And when the woman saw that the tree was good for food, and that it was pleasant to the eyes, and a tree to be desired to make one wise, she took of the fruit thereof, and did eat, and gave also unto her husband with her; and he did eat.*

Satan succeeded in deceiving Eve and having Adam join her in their rebellion against God, thereby following the rebel, Satan. However, it was still possible for mankind to be redeemed, and this God proceeded to do. At the same time, Satan became the god of this world, and established his kingdom built on the principle of "me first." Adam fell because he was not satisfied to be the "image-bearer" of the Creator, but to displace the Creator Himself.

Basic Biblical Concepts:

Sin, Suffering and Persecution

After the fall, sin brought both suffering and death. The woman will experience pain in childbirth and be subjected to a strain in her relationship with her husband, where she seeks to control him instead of allowing him to rule. The man was created to be able to work. However, now his work will be frustrated and accompanied by pain. Ultimately, his work will cease because of death. However, death is an act of mercy to prevent sin from multiplying out of control if men were to live eternally with a sin nature. The woman's fulfillment also would be limited by death. The snake, of course, was cursed to crawl on its belly and eat the dust of the earth.

Satan will ultimately suffer the loss of his relationship with God and eventual eternal punishment in hell. The serpent will be defeated by the seed of the woman, but the redeemer will suffer pain in the process. And God Himself suffered willingly, because suffering and death are the cost of redemption and restoration of mankind to Himself. But redemption would also bring Him great glory.

When God gave us free will, He gave us freedom to worship and obey Him personally and in relationship with others. In addition to the freedom to worship with others, we have a will that is free to choose to do what is right. Often, however, we choose the wrong because we are sinners with a sin nature.

The fall of Adam into sin has adversely affected our full expression of religious freedom. We long to have unrestricted freedom of worship in propagation of our faith. Often, however, the freedom of worship results in persecution. Religious freedom without persecution is a good thing. However, in a fallen world, the righteous will be persecuted. Lack of persecution can be good, but it can also indicate that the believer has backed off in his witness to a hostile world.

Basic Biblical Concepts:

Rights and Persecution

What about our rights? There is a difference between public rights and private rights. We may be called upon to give up some of our private rights. However, we should fight for public rights, even when we are willing to yield our personal rights. Furthermore, although we may give up our own personal rights voluntarily, this does not mean that we should insist upon others giving up their rights for the sake of Christ. Sometimes Paul used his rights of Roman citizenship, and other times he yielded these rights for the cause of the kingdom. We must discern what advances God's kingdom and not what advances our own plans.

Summary

When Adam chose to follow the deceiver, he chose the path that leads to death. That death is spiritual death as well as physical death. Sin and death require God to intervene for restoration of fellowship. As we experience the pain and trials in our lives, the pain that we experience points us to God, and to the eternal, where our true fulfillment lies. The price of reconciling creation to God is pain and suffering. God knew that man would spoil the universe, but in redeeming it, His glory would be seen. However, redemption would require suffering, including suffering by God Himself.

Through persecution for righteousness' sake, mankind will be tested and tried to demonstrate his worthiness for future responsibilities in heaven in his role as king and priest. Further, it does appear that the character which we develop on earth through persecution will actually be continued after death.

Religious Persecution Began Early

We find the first religious persecution early in the Bible, in Genesis chapter 4. It is a persecution resulting from the right-eousness of Abel and the unrighteousness of Cain. It began at the first recorded formal worship service. It began also in the context of the home itself.

When God confronted Cain, His choice of the words "the

voice of thy brother's blood crieth unto me from the ground" refers to all the oppressed crying out because they've been denied justice. God hears, and God judges. God's mark on Cain shows that even a murderer is not beyond God's mercy and protection. God protects the right to life, even for those who do not deserve it. Unfortunately, although Cain had the opportunity to repent and bring the right kind of offering, he resented the fact that God preferred Abel's offering and remained separated from God.

Abel, then, is the first martyr. His life still speaks of the necessity for a blood sacrifice, and that good works such as Cain performed are not sufficient. *Hebrews 11:[4] By faith Abel offered unto God a more excellent sacrifice than Cain, by which he obtained witness that he was righteous, God testifying of his gifts: and by it he being dead yet speaketh.*

Furthermore, we find a general principle. Those walking in the flesh will persecute those walking in the Spirit. *Galatians 4:[28] Now we, brethren, as Isaac was, are the children of promise.[29] But as then he that was born after the flesh persecuted him that was born after the Spirit, even so it is now.*

As we trace further in the Bible, we find that Enoch preached against the ungodly lives of those around him. *Jude [14] And Enoch also, the seventh from Adam, prophesied of these, saying, Behold, the Lord cometh with ten thousands of his saints,[15] To execute judgment upon all, and to convince all that are ungodly among them of all their ungodly deeds which they have ungodly committed, and of all their hard speeches which ungodly sinners have spoken against him.* We do not find direct persecution; God took him directly to heaven. *Hebrews 11:[5] By faith Enoch was translated that he should not see death; and was not found, because God had translated him: for before his translation he had this testimony, that he pleased God.*

Then we come to Noah, also a preacher of righteousness. His preaching fell on deaf ears. He was only assisted by his own sons in his huge work of building the ark. God judged mankind with a flood which killed everyone except the family of Noah.

A further development occurs after the flood. God delegates to mankind the responsibility of being the agents of his justice as upholders of the right to life. He places this right in the hands of the civil authorities. *Genesis 9:[5] And surely your blood of your lives will I require; at the hand of every beast will I require it, and at the hand of man; at the hand of every man's brother will I require the life of man.[6] Whoso sheddeth man's blood, by man shall his blood be shed: for in the image of God made he man.* The individual is not to take revenge independently, but through government. This responsibility has never been removed since the flood.

Further Persecution in the Pentateuch: Abraham and Lot

In the story of Lot being rescued from persecution at Sodom, we learn an interesting lesson. Persecution is not restricted to spiritual giants or mature believers. I personally had doubted if Lot was truly saved until I read what was written about him in *2 Peter 2:[7] And delivered just Lot, vexed with the filthy conversation of the wicked:[8] (For that righteous man dwelling among them, in seeing and hearing, vexed his righteous soul from day to day with their unlawful deeds;)[9] The Lord knoweth how to deliver the godly out of temptations, and to reserve the unjust unto the day of judgment to be punished.*

There we find him referred to as "righteous (just) Lot." Lot was a compromiser. Still, he was ridiculed by the godless men of Sodom, who threatened to assault him sexually. *Genesis 19:[9] And they said, Stand back. And they said again, This one fellow came in to sojourn, and he will needs be a judge: now will we deal worse with thee, than with them. And they pressed sore upon the man, even Lot, and came near to break the door.*

All who claim to follow God will be challenged to make a stand, including the compromisers. *2 Timothy 3:12. Yea, and all that will live godly in Christ Jesus shall suffer persecution.* This is a promise of God. God rescued Lot, but Lot paid dearly for his compromise. Compromise is no guarantee for protection from persecution.

In the life of Abraham, we find that true faith inevitably suffers, sacrifices, and hopes. Abraham left his family and home to travel to an unknown country. Twice his wife ended up in the harem of the ruler of the country, largely because of his lie that Sarah was his sister. He experienced disappointments, pain and tears. His greatest trial was offering Isaac, his son, to the Lord. But through his obedience, he was blessed, and all mankind with him. *Heb. 11[8] By faith Abraham, when he was called to go out into a place which he should after receive for an inheritance, obeyed; and he went out, not knowing whither he went.[9] By faith he sojourned in the land of promise, as in a strange country, dwelling in tabernacles with Isaac and Jacob, the heirs with him of the same promise:[10] For he looked for a city which hath foundations, whose builder and maker is God.[11] Through faith also Sara herself received strength to conceive seed, and was delivered of a child when she was past age, because she judged him faithful who had promised. . . [17] By faith Abraham, when he was tried, offered up Isaac: and he that had received the promises offered up his only begotten son,[18] Of whom it was said, That in Isaac shall thy seed be called:[19] Accounting that God was able to raise him up, even from the dead; from whence also he received him in a figure.*

Further Persecution in the Pentateuch: Isaac, Jacob and Joseph

Abraham's son Isaac had a number of problems with the Philistines. He was persecuted because of their envy over how the Lord had blessed him. *Genesis 26:[22] And he removed from thence, and digged another well; and for that they strove not: and he called the name of it Rehoboth; and he said, For now the LORD hath made room for us, and we shall be fruitful in the land.* However, he refused to retaliate, and the Lord continued blessing him, and the Philistines came to make a peace treaty with him. From him we learn that life may be filled with stress, opposition, and hardship. Likewise, Jacob suffered at the hands of his brother Esau and his uncle Laban, though much of his suffering resulted from his own sins and greed. It was only as he wrestled with the angel of the Lord that he became Israel, a prince with God.

We then read of Joseph, who, in a number of ways, was a type of Christ. He was somewhat proud and indiscreet and suffered at the hands of his unrighteous brothers. God used his trials over the next 13 years, both in Potiphar's house and in prison, to develop the character he needed. Joseph yielded to God and trusted him throughout these trials, and God was then able to use him greatly to save his people. When his brothers thought he would take revenge, he refused to do so. *Genesis 50:[20] But as for you, ye thought evil against me; but God meant it unto good, to bring to pass, as it is this day, to save much people alive.*

Many have observed that access to power often brings the individual to misuse the power for his own desires. We seldom see a dictator who does not abuse his power. But Joseph did not, but blessed his own people as well as the Egyptians for 80 years as the most powerful leader under Pharoah when Egypt was the dominant world power.

Further Persecution in the Pentateuch: Israel Persecuted in Egypt and Suffering in the Wilderness

As we look towards the relationship of Israel and Egypt, we find that Israel suffered because they are God's people. Moses chose a life of hardship to liberate his people and suffered both from the Egyptians and from the Israelites themselves. *Hebrews 11:[24] By faith Moses, when he was come to years, refused to be called the son of Pharaoh's daughter;[25] Choosing rather to*

23

suffer affliction with the people of God, than to enjoy the pleasures of sin for a season;[26] Esteeming the reproach of Christ greater riches than the treasures in Egypt: for he had respect unto the recompence of the reward.[27] By faith he forsook Egypt, not fearing the wrath of the king: for he endured, as seeing him who is invisible.

God worked in the life of Moses so that he was rescued from a certain death in the Nile River. He was raised with all the skills and learning of the Egyptians since he was raised as the son of Pharaoh's daughter. He spent his first 40 years primarily raised as an Egyptian prince although he was aware of his Hebrew background. Moses fled from Egypt into the wilderness after killing an Egyptian. God worked in his life for 40 years in the wilderness with the simple life of a shepherd, which was an abomination in the sight of the Egyptians. He returned to confront the new Pharoah and spend the last 40 years of his life leading Israel toward the promised land. He had many trials and hardships while traveling through the wilderness, including rebellion against him from the very Israelites whom he led. God met with him and conformed him to perhaps the greatest leader in the Old Testament. His problems thrust him to have a close relationship with God and changed his character.

Other Insights in the Pentateuch

Every good gift comes from God. Many blessings or curses result from man's response to God. We find this especially true in Deuteronomy 28. Some blessings and curses are also a result of God's plan for man. This is especially true in the life of Joseph. Blessings can become curses if we fail to glorify God through them. Joseph responded appropriately and experienced, at last, the blessing of God. In the long term, the sow-reap principle generally holds, but often it does not hold in the short term. Suffering is a part of God's plan, used for chastisement to bring His people to Himself. We must trust God in all circumstances and allow Him to work in our lives. Sometimes suffering is the result of our own sins. Suffering then can lead to repentance and the glory of God. An example would be Zaccheus, who stopped extorting the people and paid back fourfold those he had robbed. As we yield to God, suffering can change the character of the sufferer to become transformed into the image of Jesus. And, praise the Lord, we know that ultimately sin and suffering are not permanent, and we will be free from both in heaven.

Suffering in Judges

As we trace Israel's history forward, we see that God often used suffering in His people to bring them back to Himself. The book of Judges has seven cycles showing this truth. God blessed His people, and also warned them, especially through Moses in the book of Deuteronomy. They were not to consider blessings as evidence of their own intrinsic goodness and were not to leave the worship of the true God. However, when the people would begin to live in luxury and become prideful, God would permit a disaster to occur, usually in the form of oppression from an enemy. The people would suffer. Eventually they would cry out to Him, and He would provide a deliverer, who would bring them to the area of blessing. Once again, they would begin to live in luxury and become prideful, and the cycle would repeat itself.

Judges 2:[16] Nevertheless the LORD raised up judges, which delivered them out of the hand of those that spoiled them.[17] And yet they would not hearken unto their judges, but they went a whoring after other gods, and bowed themselves unto them: they turned quickly out of the way which their fathers walked in, obeying the commandments of the LORD; but they did not so.[18] And when the LORD raised them up judges, then the LORD was with the judge, and delivered them out of the hand of their enemies all the days of the judge: for it repented the LORD because of their groanings by reason of them that oppressed them and vexed them.[19] And it came to pass, when the judge was dead, that they returned, and corrupted themselves more than their fathers, in following other gods to serve them, and to bow down unto them; they ceased not from their own doings, nor from their stubborn way.[20] And the anger of the LORD was hot against Israel; and he said, Because that this people hath transgressed my covenant which I commanded their fathers, and have not hearkened unto my voice;[21] I also will not henceforth drive out any from before them of the nations which Joshua left when he died:[22] That through them I may prove Israel, whether they will keep the way of the LORD to walk therein, as their fathers did keep it, or not.

The men we call judges were really military leaders who led the people to freedom. Sometimes the people would truly repent and return to the Lord, and the Lord would allow them victory. We can see a similar pattern in the lives of many of the kings. The victory, however, was temporary. Pride would arise, and the nation would ignore God or rebel against Him. The enemies were really used as His instruments to correct His period.

Job

When we come to the book of Job, we find new insights. The book begins with Job, the most righteous man on earth, being praised by the God of heaven. Before the host of heaven, Satan directly challenges God by stating that Job does not serve God because He is God, but only because he receives riches from God. God accepts the challenge and gives Satan the opportunity to remove Job's riches. Thus Job is allowed to suffer because of his righteousness to see if he will curse God when his riches are removed. Satan removes Job's goods and family, and yet Job blesses God. In the second round, Satan again accuses Job of not truly loving God, but worshiping Him because he still has his health. Again, God gives Satan a chance to test Job, and Job ends up with painful stinking boils from head to foot, sitting on an ash heap outside of town. Even his own wife tells him to curse God and die. However, Job reproves her and does not curse God.

Job's three friends arrive, and horrified at his condition, sit in sorrow with him for a full week. So far, so good. But unfortunately, they feel that they must advise Job as to the cause of his troubles. We can learn from his friends that suffering people need our presence more than our advice. Sometimes by our advice, we actually intensify their problems. Job's friends all believed that he was sinning, and that if he would repent, his fortunes would be restored. However, they were wrong. Job maintained his innocence, and his friends simply aggravated his pain. Thus, there is a mystery to suffering, and often we do not know why suffering occurs. Job longed for a mediator, but there was no mediator which he could see.

God finally answered Job. He did not answer the question "why," but the question "who." It is Almighty God who has permitted his suffering. Do we trust Him? We have already learned that some suffering is due to sin in our lives, and it is a corrective to bring us back to God. This is true particularly in the book of Judges and with the various kings of Israel. Suffering is sometimes part of God's plan to develop character in our lives, as in the life of Joseph. But here we see that suffering can be a witness to the faithfulness of the true believer and the worthiness of God. This witness is not only to mankind, but also to the hosts of heaven.

If God does not show us of what repent; if He does not point out the sin in our lives, then correction is probably not His goal for our suffering. Punishment without conviction is vindictive, as is punishment after confession and repentance. Both are against the nature of our God. Thus, we should go before God, seeking His face and asking the Holy Spirit to examine our hearts and lives. If God does not convict of sin, or if sincere confession and repentance does not remedy the situation, then probably something else is going on. At that point, we need to love and trust God, knowing that this response will reveal the accusations of Satan as lies.

It is ironic that Job's friends themselves were called on to repent, but they had not suffered. Job spoke rightly about God and did suffer. Again, we are reminded that all who would live godly shall suffer persecution, and that sometimes there is a certain mystery in suffering. Job's suffering was the direct result of his faithfulness to God. This is against the so-called Word of Faith teachings. If we insist on finding the meaning of every isolated event or trial, we will make mistakes. We cannot see the big picture, but God does. For example, we could make many mistakes in analyzing Joseph's situation until we see the end result of Joseph ruling over the entire land of Egypt. Most of us would never have suspected how Satan challenged the Lord until it was revealed to us in Job.

Persecution and Suffering in the Psalms

As we continue in the wisdom literature, the Psalms are a rich source of material concerning persecution. The Jews had over 1000 years of history of persecution and abuse prior to Christ, and the New Testament believers could look back on the Scriptures to see validation of persecution for righteousness sake. Many of the Jews had learned the Psalms since their childhood. When Jesus cried out on the cross *Psalm 22:[1] My God, my God, why hast thou forsaken me? why art thou so far from helping me, and from the words of my roaring?* some of the Jews in attendance at the crucifixion of our Lord would be able to see the truth of that Psalm being lived out before them: the gambling for the clothes, the piercing of hands and feet, and the mocking crowd. Yet, the Psalm ends with praise and thanksgiving.

We find similar truths in *Psalm 31:[5] Into thine hand I commit my spirit: thou hast redeemed me, O LORD God of truth. Jesus quoted this on the cross. We find a statement in Psalm 34:[19] Many are the afflictions of the righteous: but the LORD delivereth him out of them all. [20] He keepeth all his bones: not one of them is broken.* The righteous can expect many afflictions. But they can expect God's deliverance too. Psalm 34 also predicts that Jesus' bones will not be broken, as were the bones of the other two who were crucified. In Psalm 35, they hated

Christ without a cause, and in *Psalm 41, His own friend betrayed Him. 41:[9] Yea, mine own familiar friend, in whom I trusted, which did eat of my bread, hath lifted up his heel against me.*

Psalm 44 also shows how the righteous are persecuted: *44:[22] Yea, for thy sake are we killed all the day long; we are counted as sheep for the slaughter. Psalm 69 is quoted several times, particularly vs. [21] They gave me also gall for my meat; and in my thirst they gave me vinegar to drink.* Again, they could see that verse lived out at the cross. *Psalm 118:[22] The stone which the builders refused is become the head stone of the corner.[23] This is the LORD's doing; it is marvellous in our eyes.* These verses are quoted more often in the New Testament than any other verses in the Psalms. They are viewed as referring to the rejection of Christ - again the rejection of the righteous.

As a whole, the Psalms give us the understanding and the right words for handling a wide variety of circumstances, including persecution. They can help us to understand the persecution of the righteous, like Jesus Christ, and help us when we face persecution ourselves The imprecatory psalms, which cry for punishment of the wicked, are also a cry for divine justice. God is not shocked with the strong feelings of the persecuted. But the psalms do not advise the individual himself to do the punishing, but for God to punish. Actually, these psalms may remind us to confess our own sins when we are unrighteous. And many view these psalms as the actual prayers of our sinless High Priest on our behalf.

Persecution and Suffering in Other Wisdom Literature

Ecclesiastes shows that life on earth does not always make sense. It shows that sometimes right does not prevail and on earth the righteous are not always rewarded. That is reality - but there is a God in heaven who will eventually make everything right. Likewise, Proverbs reminds us that the righteous can expect persecution in this fallen world. *Proverbs 29:[10] The bloodthirsty hate the upright: but the just seek his soul.*

Furthermore, we have a responsibility to help the weak and helpless. *Proverbs 29:[7] The righteous considereth the cause of the poor: but the wicked regardeth not to know it.* There is further advice for kings, but also for everyone. *Proverbs 31:[4] It is not for kings, O Lemuel, it is not for kings to drink wine; nor for princes strong drink:[5] Lest they drink, and forget the law, and pervert the judgment of any of the afflicted....[8] Open thy mouth for the dumb in the cause of all such as are appointed to destruction.[9] Open thy mouth, judge righteously, and plead the cause of the poor and needy.*

Further Old Testament Examples of Individuals Suffering for Righteousness Sake

We find a number of examples in the Old Testament of individuals suffering for righteousness sake. This was true for Abel. It is particularly true for the prophets. Here is a short list of some persecuted for righteousness sake:[7]

1. Moses threatened with stoning by his own people

2. David threatened by Saul on several occasions

3. 85 priests of Nob killed by Doeg and Saul

4. Many prophets hunted and killed by Jezebel

5. Elijah persecuted by Ahab & Jezebel

6. Micaiah imprisoned by King Ahab

7. Elisha threatened by death by the king

8. Hanani imprisoned by King Asa

9. Zachariah stoned at the order of King Joas

10. Jeremiah suffered greatly from both kings and false prophets

11. Uriah the prophet is caught and executed

12. Manasseh killed much innocent blood - traditionally Isaiah the prophet is one of those he killed

13. Daniel, Shadrach, Meshach and Abednego - we will look at them later

Persecution and the Prophets

Jesus looked at Himself in line with the prophets. He was called a great prophet. And He spoke these words to the religious leaders: *Luke 11:[47] Woe unto you! for ye build the sepulchres of the prophets, and your fathers killed them...[49] Therefore also said the wisdom of God, I will send them prophets and apostles, and some of them they shall slay and persecute:[50] That the blood of all the prophets, which was shed from the foundation of the world, may be required of this generation;* Many of the prophets suffered for righteousness sake. Both Elijah and Elisha suffered, although God used them greatly. However, we will focus on Isaiah, Jeremiah and Daniel.

Isaiah

The prophet Isaiah shows us several purposes for suffering. Suffering can be punishment for sin. An example of this would be the destruction of the Assyrian army and death of Sennacharib. Suffering may be discipline for training and education. An example would be the abscess of Hezekiah which God healed through a plaster. Suffering may help us establish our relationship with the living God, and live for Him, as we see in the life of Job. Suffering is often how God accomplishes his purposes in the world. God works through the Suffering Servant who suffers for the sins of others. Those who would follow Him will also suffer and show self-sacrifice. *Isaiah 50:[10] Who is among you that feareth the LORD, that obeyeth the voice of his servant, that walketh in darkness, and hath no light? Let him trust in the name of the LORD, and stay upon his God.* This suffering for others often demonstrates the power of God to bring the persecutor to Himself. God often uses the sufferer who responds to his persecutor in love to change the heart of the persecutor from an enemy of God to one who accepts God's redeeming sacrifice.

Isaiah 53 shows the humiliation and exaltation of the suffering servant. *Isaiah 53:[1] Who hath believed our report? and to whom is the arm of the LORD revealed?[2] For he shall grow up before him as a tender plant, and as a root out of a dry ground: he hath no form nor comeliness; and when we shall see him, there is no beauty that we should desire him.[3] He is despised and rejected of men; a man of sorrows, and acquainted with grief: and we hid as it were our faces from him; he was despised, and we esteemed him not.[4] Surely he hath borne our griefs, and carried our sorrows: yet we did esteem him stricken, smitten of God, and afflicted.[5] But he was wounded for our transgressions, he was bruised for our iniquities: the chastisement of our peace was upon him; and with his stripes we are healed.[6] All we like sheep have gone astray; we have turned every one to his own way; and the LORD hath laid on him the iniquity of us all. [7] He was oppressed, and he was afflicted, yet he opened not his mouth: he is brought as a lamb to the slaughter, and as a sheep before her shearers is dumb, so he openeth not his mouth.[8] He was taken from prison and from judgment: and who shall declare his generation? for he was cut off out of the land of the living: for the transgression of my people was he stricken.[9] And he made his grave with the wicked, and with the rich in his death; because he had done no violence, neither was any deceit in his mouth.*

But ultimately the Servant, who is clearly the Lord Jesus Christ, will be exalted. *Isaiah 53:[10] Yet it pleased the LORD to bruise him; he hath put him to grief: when thou shalt make his soul an offering for sin, he shall see his seed, he shall prolong his days, and the pleasure of the LORD shall prosper in his hand.[11] He shall see of the travail of his soul, and shall be satisfied: by his knowledge shall my righteous servant justify many; for he shall bear their iniquities.[12] Therefore will I divide him a portion with the great, and he shall divide the spoil with the strong; because he hath poured out his soul unto death: and he was numbered with the transgressors; and he bare the sin of many, and made intercession for the transgressors.* Again, we see the righteous suffer for the unrighteous, but God will eventually raise up and glorify the righteous Son of God.

Jeremiah

The prophet Jeremiah faced a great deal of persecution. He preached against the hypocrisy of the nation during the last 20 years of the reign of good king Josiah without persecution. But after the death of Josiah, and especially after the ascension of wicked King Johoiakim, he was severely persecuted. He was opposed by his own family, by the people of Jerusalem, by the false prophets, by the corrupt priests, and by the princes and kings of Judah. He was jailed, and on one occasion he was thrown into a pit and sank into the muddy bottom. It took thirty men to pull him out. Worse than the physical punishment was the mocking he faced because he was preaching the word of God. Nevertheless, he had an intense love for his people.

Jeremiah knew from the beginning that his message would be rejected. At one point, he wanted to resign from his task as a prophet but could not because of God's Word burning in his life. But God promised to be with him, and that He would not forsake him. Because he believed that he was preaching the words of God, Jeremiah understood that the people were not rejecting him, but they were rejecting the living God. He preached faithfully for 40 years, and when his prophecies were fulfilled, he grieved both for his people and with his people. We see his grief especially in the book of Lamentations.

Daniel

The prophet Daniel also gives us a number of insights. God is sovereign in history, and He will fulfill His promises. God also shares his authority with man. But we must remain faithful unto death. God will test us. Those people who are faithful unto death are the kind of people that God will trust to rule over the nations.

They will obey God and live by his laws despite the cost. They will be faithful through trials, persecutions, and threats of death.

Daniel and his friends were tested with the requirement that they partake of the king's food, which was probably offered to idols and broke a number of the Jewish dietary commandments. Later, Shadrach, Meshach and Abednego faced death in the fiery oven but they would not deny their God to save their lives. In the same way, Daniel would rather face the lion's den than to neglect prayer to the living God even though he was an old man.

These men proclaimed and honored the sovereign rule of God in everything. They were immersed in the task of telling others about God and leading them to Him. They knew that the loss of temporal goods or even life itself for God's sake is not loss but is gain. They recognized that their true fulfillment was in eternity. God tested these men with their worldly goods, position and even their lives. They were victorious in the tests. These men and others like them will reign with God and under God throughout eternity.

Daniel, at the conclusion of his book, showed that he believed in the resurrection of the righteous to eternal life and the lost to eternal damnation. Notice these words in *Daniel 7:[26] But the judgment shall sit, and they shall take away his dominion, to consume and to destroy it unto the end.[27] And the kingdom and dominion, and the greatness of the kingdom under the whole heaven, shall be given to the people of the saints of the most High, whose kingdom is an everlasting kingdom, and all dominions shall serve and obey him.* Thus, in the long run, there are great rewards to those who are faithful to God.

Esther

The book of Esther clearly demonstrates persecution of the righteous. Mordecai the Jew shows himself to be totally loyal to God and to the king. His niece Esther becomes the new queen. When Mordecai fails to bow to Haman the Agagite, Haman not only wants to kill Mordecai but eliminate the entire Jewish race.

Although God is not mentioned directly in the book, we see the hand of God in the entire book as Esther and Mordecai foil the plans of Haman, and see their rights vindicated. Esther is willing to risk her life for her people. "If I perish, I perish," she proclaims.

On the other hand, we see many who failed the test. Several individuals demonstrated that they could not be trusted with power and authority without misusing it. Ahab and Jezebel failed to use their position to honor God but killed the righteous Naboth. David, the anointed of God, spared Saul's life twice. But later he ordered the execution of righteous Uriah to cover up David's sin with his wife, Bathsheba. Asa jailed the faithful prophet Hanani. Manasseh killed many innocent victims including the prophet Isaiah. Joash ordered his followers to execute Zachariah, the high priest and the son of the very man who saved his life as a child. Zachariah's "crime" was faithfully telling the king to stop his idolatry.

The Intertestamental Period and Persecution Under Antiochus Epiphanes

The intertestamental period included a time of incredible suffering for faithful Jews. Antiochus Epiphanes took power over Israel and decided to remove all traces of the Jewish faith and hellenize the country to Greek heathen beliefs. He tortured many Jews, forcing them to eat pork. He made circumcision a crime punishable by death. When two Jewish women were found who had circumcised their babies, the babies were tied around their necks, and they were thrown off the city wall to their deaths. One Jewish woman had seven sons tortured horribly one by one, but they refused to deny the Mosaic rules.[8] She encouraged them to be faithful unto death. During this time, the Jews resolved the question of why the righteous suffer by recognizing a judgment after death and resurrection and reward to the faithful.

35

General Comments on Persecution and Suffering in the Old Testament

God is able to relate to those who suffer. He is not an impassive, unfeeling God, sitting high above the earth with no compassion, looking indifferently at our suffering. That is the picture of Buddha, who was detached from the world. Jesus Christ came as a suffering servant. Jesus Christ entered a suffering world. He entered into our sorrows and suffering, hunger, thirst, and weariness. Because it was the Father's will, He willingly went to the cross. *Hebrews 5:[7] Who in the days of his flesh, when he had offered up prayers and supplications with strong crying and tears unto him that was able to save him from death, and was heard in that he feared; [8] Though he were a Son, yet learned he obedience by the things which he suffered;*

The cross is central in revealing the nature of God. In the incarnation, God Himself suffers. Even in the Old Testament, God suffers in His interaction with man. The cross reveals that God Himself has entered our world of suffering and suffered both with us and for us.

When God looked at the sins of the world, He was grieved. He was grieved before the flood. *Genesis 6:[6] And it repented the LORD that he had made man on the earth, and it grieved him at his heart.* He was grieved by Israel in the wilderness wanderings. *Psalm 78:[40] How oft did they provoke him in the wilderness, and grieve him in the desert![41] Yea, they turned back and tempted God, and limited the Holy One of Israel.* The Holy Spirit is grieved. *Isaiah 63:[10] But they rebelled, and vexed his holy Spirit: therefore he was turned to be their enemy, and he fought against them.*

Jesus was sorrowed and grieved over Jerusalem. *Mt. 23:[37] O Jerusalem, Jerusalem, thou that killest the prophets, and stonest them which are sent unto thee, how often would I have gathered thy children together, even as a hen gathereth her chickens under her wings, and ye would not!* Jesus was sorrowed at Saul's persecution of Christians. *Acts 9:[4] And he fell to the earth, and heard a voice saying unto him, Saul, Saul, why persecutest thou me?* God feels our pain. Jesus knows. *Heb. 4:[15] For we have not an high priest which cannot be touched with the feeling of our infirmities; but was in all points tempted like as we are, yet without sin.[16] Let us therefore come boldly unto the throne of grace, that we may obtain mercy, and find grace to help in time of need.* Notice the Lord's words: Why persecutest thou me?

The Trinity is giving and receiving from each other, depending on each other, and offering themselves to each other. God completes His plans not by force or power, but by love and self-giving: the cross. The self-giving God persuades and invites; He does not force. Jesus Christ came as an offering, and a sacrifice, which reveals the true nature of God. He shows how God's people should live as well. *Philippians 2:[3] Let nothing be done through strife or vainglory; but in lowliness of mind let each esteem other better than themselves. [4] Look not every man on his own things, but every man also on the things of others. [5] Let this mind be in you, which was also in Christ Jesus: [6] Who, being in the form of God, thought it not robbery to be equal with God: [7] But made himself of no reputation, and took upon him the form of a servant, and was made in the likeness of men: [8] And being found in fashion as a man, he humbled himself, and became obedient unto death, even the death of the cross.*

We need to be careful how we present the gospel. If our motives are unworthy, our glory will become manifest rather than God's glory. If our methods are unworthy, we will resort to coercion by physical means, moral constraint, or psychological pressure. If our message is unworthy, we will misrepresent the Lord Jesus Christ. God never uses force, but rather persuasion. Even in the face of heresy, the Christian must use persuasion, and not force. Truth will ultimately triumph over error. (We see this later in the clash between Arius and Athanasius. Arius prevailed initially, claiming that Jesus was the son of God, but not God the Son, actually God come in the flesh. Athanasius disagreed and was deposed from his position as bishop on multiple occasions. Yet Athanasius was eventually vindicated.)

God's people not only suffer for their *faith*, but they also suffer for *Him*. They suffer for the fulfillment of His purposes in the world. They are in the line of the prophets. They are not just stoic, but they rejoice and love those who persecute them. Like God gives light and rain to those who curse Him, so we are to bless those who persecute us. We are in service to those who cause us to suffer. Jesus makes great promises to those who suffer for him. We are the possessors of the kingdom of heaven. Suffering for the kingdom is expected from all of God's messengers. This is a sign that God is actually present in the ministry. Persecution is inevitable. Sometimes, persecutors will silence the message, but many times they will not be satisfied without silencing the messenger of the gospel as well.

Pastor Hsi was effective in communicating the gospel when Korea was torn by the communists in the 1950's. A young radical communist ended up shooting his two oldest sons to death while all three were in the university. Pastor Hsi sent his daughter to the court to plead with the judge to place the young man under his jurisdiction. This was done, and through his love and forgiveness, the young man came to Christ and became a pastor also. Another example of the power of the gospel was shown by a lady in China who was unmercifully persecuted by the communist boss of the town. She was consigned to cleaning the open gutters of human waste. When the wife of the boss became critically ill, no one would help until finally this lady offered to care for her. Her love won the communist leader to Christ.

Persecution in the New Testament

The Jewish nation did not recognize Jesus as their messiah. Those who had years of contact with Him in Nazareth, where he was raised, did not recognize Him as the promised anointed one. When he went to the synagogue in Nazareth, He was given the scripture to read, and read Isaiah 61:1-2 and said that He fulfilled the prophecy. He commented: *Luke 4:24 And he said: Verily I say unto you, No prophet is accepted in his own country...* He then gave two illustrations, that of Elijah going to a widow outside of Israel to minister to her while a great famine was going on, and Elisha healing Naaman the Syrian general from Syria – showing that God was interested in all people and not the Jews. They were so incensed that they tried to kill Him by throwing him over a hill, but He simply passed through their midst. Again, after speaking the parables of the mystery kingdom in Matthew 13, He went to the synagogue (Matthew 13:54-58). They were astonished and said: *"Whence hath this man this wisdom, and these mighty works? Is not this the carpenter's son? Is not his mother called Mary? And his brethren James, and Joses, and Simon, and Judas? And his sisters, are they not all with us? Whence then hath this man all these things?" And they were offended in him. But Jesus said unto them: "A prophet is not without honor, save in his own country, and in his own house." And he did not many mighty works there because of their unbelief.*

In the New Testament, the Jews were waiting for the anointed one, the Messiah. They had a wide variety of ideas about Him. They looked for a king or king-priest who would restore Israel and bring the country into a proper relationship with God. Jesus asked His disciples this very question. *Mt. 16:[13] When Jesus came into the coasts of Caesarea Philippi, he asked his disciples, saying, Whom do men say that I the Son of man am?[14] And they said, Some say that thou art John the Baptist: some, Elias; and others, Jeremias, or one of the prophets.[15] He saith unto them, But whom say ye that I am?[16] And Simon Peter answered and said, Thou art the Christ, the Son of the living God.[17] And Jesus answered and said unto him, Blessed art thou, Simon Barjona: for flesh and blood hath not revealed it unto thee, but my Father which is in heaven.[18] And I say also unto thee, That thou art Peter, and upon this rock I will build my church; and the gates of hell shall not prevail against it.[19] And I will give unto thee the keys of the kingdom of heaven: and whatsoever thou shalt bind on earth shall be bound in heaven: and whatsoever thou shalt loose on earth shall be loosed in heaven.[20] Then charged he his disciples that they should tell no man that he was Jesus the Christ.*

At this point, Jesus revealed what was involved in being the Messiah. *Mt. 16:[21] From that time forth began Jesus to shew unto his disciples, how that he must go unto Jerusalem, and suffer many things of the elders and chief priests and scribes, and be killed, and be raised again the third day.[22] Then Peter took him, and began to rebuke him, saying, Be it far from thee, Lord: this shall not be unto thee.[23] But he turned, and said unto Peter, Get thee behind me, Satan: thou art an offence unto me: for thou savourest not the things that be of God, but those that be of men.* Jesus revealed that the Messiah must die. When Peter objected, Jesus recalled the same temptation from Satan in the wilderness to bypass suffering and the cross, and He rebuked Peter. Peter was thinking man's thoughts, not God's thoughts. Peter's suggestion for Christ to avoid the cross was the same suggestion Satan had made in the wilderness. The suggestion to save yourself is actually satanic and leads to losing your life.

Jesus then went on to reveal that the same fate was in store for those who truly followed Him as disciples. *Mt. 16:[24] Then said Jesus unto his disciples, If any man will come after me, let him deny himself, and take up his cross, and follow me.[25] For whosoever will save his life shall lose it: and whosoever will lose his life for my sake shall find it.[26] For what is a man profited, if he shall gain the whole world, and lose his own soul? or what shall a man give in exchange for his soul? [27] For the Son of man shall come in the glory of his Father with his angels; and then he shall reward every man according to his works.* Thus, the disciple can expect persecution and even martyrdom as he follows Christ. He will receive rewards, but not until Jesus returns at the second coming.

Jesus had predicted His own death many times but, even though the disciples had received reassurance at the transfiguration, at the time of crucifixion, they abandoned Him. Even after His resurrection but before His ascension, they questioned if He would restore Israel at that time. But instead, He sent them into the world as His witnesses.

The Jews had difficulty accepting Jesus as the Messiah, and even John the Baptist wondered. They expected a conquering king, but Jesus worked through weakness, poverty, humility, and ultimately through the cross. John had stated clearly that he was not the Messiah, and the following day identified Jesus as the Messiah. *Jn. 1:[19] And this is the record of John, when the Jews sent priests and Levites from Jerusalem to ask him, Who art thou?[20] And he confessed, and denied not; but confessed, I am not the Christ.[21] And they asked him, What then? Art thou Elias? And he saith, I am not. Art thou that prophet? And he answered, No.[22] Then said they unto him, Who art thou? that we may give an answer to them that sent us. What sayest thou of thyself?[23] He said, I am the voice of one crying in the wilderness, Make straight the way of the Lord, as said the prophet Esaias.[24] And they which were sent were of the Pharisees.[25] And they asked him, and said unto him, Why baptizest thou then, if thou be not that Christ, nor Elias, neither that prophet?[26] John answered them, saying, I baptize with water: but there standeth one among you, whom ye know not;[27] He it is, who coming after me is preferred before me, whose shoe's latchet I am not worthy to unloose.[28] These things were done in Bethabara beyond Jordan, where John was baptizing.[29] The next day John seeth Jesus coming unto him, and saith, Behold the Lamb of God, which taketh away the sin of the world.[30] This is he of whom I said, After me cometh a man which is preferred before me: for he was before me.*

John heard the voice from heaven when he baptized Jesus. He testified for Jesus. *Jn. 3:[27] John answered and said, A man*

41

can receive nothing, except it be given him from heaven.[28] Ye yourselves bear me witness, that I said, I am not the Christ, but that I am sent before him.[29] He that hath the bride is the bridegroom: but the friend of the bridegroom, which standeth and heareth him, rejoiceth greatly because of the bridegroom's voice: this my joy therefore is fulfilled.[30] He must increase, but I must decrease. But later he sent his disciples to ask about Jesus while he was in prison. Jesus' methods were different from what he had anticipated. Jesus answered by performing many miracles and healings among the multitude, fulfilling what the prophets had written about the messiah. He sent John's prophets back to tell him what they had seen. Then he praised John before the multitude. Even John had difficulty visualizing a suffering messiah.

The Beatitudes and Suffering

In the beatitudes, Jesus shows His disciples the characteristics that they should develop. These characteristics are present within true believers in the kingdom. They are those who are poor in spirit, those who mourn, the meek, those who hunger and thirst after righteousness, the merciful, the pure in heart, and the peacemakers. Most striking, however, is the revelation that those are blessed who are persecuted for doing right. *Mt. 5:[10] Blessed are they which are persecuted for righteousness' sake: for theirs is the kingdom of heaven.[11] Blessed are ye, when men shall revile you, and persecute you, and shall say all manner of evil against you falsely, for my sake.[12] Rejoice, and be exceeding glad: for great is your reward in heaven: for so persecuted they the prophets which were before you.*

Jesus Teaches Five Principles

1. Suffering is for His sake. Men suffer not for their faith, but because of their allegiance to His priorities and standards —they suffer for Him.

2. Those who suffer for Him are in line with the prophets, God's messengers to the world.

3. The disciples must not merely be stoic but rejoice and love those who persecute them. The persecuted are in service to the persecutors, and they are to bless those who curse them.

4. There are tremendous promises to grasp. Disciples are partakers of the kingdom of heaven. But they may experience ridicule, persecution and slander as they witness to the world.

5. Persecution is inevitable. Sometimes the world will move past ridicule to violent rejection of the message and often violently reject the messenger as well.

The message is reinforced at the end of *Matthew 5:[43] Ye have heard that it hath been said, Thou shalt love thy neighbour, and hate thine enemy.[44] But I say unto you, Love your enemies, bless them that curse you, do good to them that hate you, and pray for them which despitefully use you, and persecute you;[45] That ye may be the children of your Father which is in heaven: for he maketh his sun to rise on the evil and on the good, and sendeth rain on the just and on the unjust.[46] For if ye love them which love you, what reward have ye? do not even the publicans the same?[47] And if ye salute your brethren only, what do ye more than others? do not even the publicans so?[48] Be ye therefore perfect, even as your Father which is in heaven is perfect.*

The Disciples of Jesus and Persecution

In Matthew 10, Jesus sent out His 12 disciples. In preparing them for this task, Jesus shows us a number of principles about persecution. Mission and persecution go together. In mission work, there is always the shadow of the cross. Jesus Himself sends us as defenseless sheep into the midst of wolves but our survival is not the key issue. Remember that Jesus Himself was like a sheep brought to the slaughter. Dangers can come in at least two directions. First, we can fear the persecution and compromise. Secondly, we must be careful that we do not deliberately provoke authorities and attract persecution. We need God's wisdom through the Holy Spirit to be wise as serpents and harmless as doves.[9]

God promises to give us wisdom to know how to speak in times of trial and persecution. *Matthew 10:19] But when they deliver you up, take no thought how or what ye shall speak: for it shall be given unto you in the same hour what ye shall speak. [20] For it is not ye that speak, but the Spirit of your Father which speaketh in you.* Many have testified to the truth of those words. We find this true with Peter and John speaking so boldly before the Sanhedrin that they are amazed that unlettered men could answer so well. They took note that they had been with Jesus. Stephen was given the right words at his defense. Jozef Ton, quoted several times above, was questioned repeatedly by the Romanian secret police. He was amazed at how God gave him the right words to say.

Jesus goes on to warn us that even family may turn against us. *Mt. 10:[21] And the brother shall deliver up the brother to death, and the father the child: and the children shall rise up against their parents, and cause them to be put to death.[22] And ye shall be hated of all men for my name's sake: but he that endureth to the end shall be saved.* The church is God's primary agent of change in the world. We become sons and daughters of him. We must not allow our ties with our biological family to take precedence over our relationship with the Lord Jesus Christ.

In Mark 3:31-35, Jesus shows that the spiritual family of obedience is more important than our biological family. *Mark 3:[31] There came his brethren and his mother, and, standing without, sent unto him, calling him. [32] And the multitude sat about him, and they said unto him, behold, thy mother and thy brethren without seek for thee. [33] And he answered them, saying, who is my mother, or my brother? [34]And he looked around on them which sat about him, and said, behold my mother and my brethren! [35] For whosoever shall do the will of God, the same is my brother, my sister, and my mother.*

In Luke 21:16-19, Jesus shows that persecution cannot separate the disciples from the care and love of God. They may suffer but are not ultimately destroyed. They must hold fast to the end. Persecution will often expose faith that is only mental assent. These people will turn back, but true faith endures to the end. *Luke 21:16] And ye shall be betrayed both by parents and brethren, and kinsfolks, and friends, and some of you shall they cause to be put to death. [17] And ye shall be hated of all men for my name's sake. [18] But there shall not a hair of your head perish. [19] In your patience, possess ye your souls.*

Jesus warns that we sometimes need to flee persecution. *Mt. 10:[22] And ye shall be hated of all men for my name's sake: but he that endureth to the end shall be saved.[23] But when they persecute you in this city, flee ye into another: for verily I say unto you, Ye shall not have gone over the cities of Israel, till the Son of man be come.* Biblical responses to persecution include flight from the persecution, as well as fortitude to bear persecution, and, on occasion, fighting against persecution. We must not flee just to avoid suffering. The priority is on the mission of the kingdom of God above all else. We are commanded by Jesus to spread the word.

Paul himself occasionally avoided persecution by flight. He mentions how he was let down in a basket over the wall at Damascus. He was warned about persecution and fled to other cities on occasion. Even the Roman government gave him protection when a group of Jews wanted to assassinate him en route to Jerusalem. Martyrdom can provide witness, but it may be better to stay alive to proclaim it. Martyrdom occurs once, but it cannot be repeated if it leads to death. True martyrdom is not something that can be repeated on multiple occasions. Jesus himself hid Himself on several occasions, or simply walked away through the crowds without being stopped. His time had not yet come.

But we must not run when obedience to God's command would be jeopardized. Thus, it is biblical to show fortitude,

45

standing firm until death. It is also biblical to fight occasionally for your legal rights. Paul did this on several occasions, but he made sure it did not hinder the furtherance of the gospel. He insisted that the authorities come to release him out of the jail at Philippi. I believe this was to protect the new believers. He claimed his Roman citizenship to prevent being flogged by the Roman authorities, and also demanded to be tried by Caesar. Sometimes, civil disobedience within guidelines is an option. Peter and John were commanded not to preach in the name of Jesus Christ. However, they said that they must obey God rather than man. They took the punishment rather than disobey God.

We can expect opposition, slander, and persecution. *Mt. 10:[24] The disciple is not above his master, nor the servant above his lord.[25] It is enough for the disciple that he be as his master, and the servant as his lord. If they have called the master of the house Beelzebub, how much more shall they call them of his household?* When I was first saved, I thought that the more I was like Jesus, the less likelihood there was for persecution. That is not true. The world rejected Jesus, and the world has not changed its attitude - it will reject those disciples who resemble Him. But this is not cause to be silent and not to witness.

Jesus commands us in *Matthew 10:[26] Fear them not therefore: for there is nothing covered, that shall not be revealed, and hid, that shall not be known. [27] What I tell you in darkness, that shall ye speak in the light: and what ye hear in the ear, that preach ye upon the housetops.* We need to speak openly for Christ. Penner makes a very strong statement: "In the midst of persecution, however, only two options are open to the follower of Christ: to confess Him or deny Him (either actively or passively.) Christ's witnesses do not have survival as their main concern. They cannot be silent. They can only be silenced."[10]

Matthew 10:[28] And fear not them which kill the body, but are not able to kill the soul: but rather fear him which is able to destroy both soul and body in hell. 29] Are not two sparrows sold for farthing? And one of them shall not fall on the ground without your father. [30] But the very hairs of your head are all numbered. [31] Fear ye not therefore, ye are more value than many sparrows. [32] Whosoever therefore shall confess me before men, him will I confess before my Father, which is in heaven. [33] But whosoever shall deny me before men, him will I also deny before my Father which is in heaven.

Jesus shows us that the danger lies not in the judgment of man, but in the judgment of God. The danger is not in the death of the body, but the eternal destruction of body and soul. Those who are afraid of men have no fear of God, and those who have fear of God have no fear of man.[11] The power of killers is limited to destruction of the body. Since God will bring the body back to life, the power of the persecutors is temporary at best. The real threat of persecution is that we may not be all that God expects of us. Penner quotes a Vietnamese pastor as saying: "Suffering is not the worst thing that can happen to us. Disobedience to God is."

We can expect that true belief will bring pain and suffering within the family itself. *Mt. 10:[34] Think not that I am come to send peace on earth: I came not to send peace, but a sword.[35] For I am come to set a man at variance against his father, and the daughter against her mother, and the daughter in law against her mother in law.[36] And a man's foes shall be they of his own household.[37] He that loveth father or mother more than me is not worthy of me: and he that loveth son or daughter more than me is not worthy of me.* We must place loyalty to Christ above loyalty to family, as painful as that may be.

We too will suffer as Jesus suffered. He was rejected by family. He was slandered and misunderstood. Ultimately, He was crucified. As we witness for Him, we will have problems too. *Mt. 10:[38] And he that taketh not his cross, and followeth after me, is not worthy of me.[39] He that findeth his life shall lose it: and he that loseth his life for my sake shall find it.[40] He that receiveth you receiveth me, and he that receiveth me*

47

receiveth him that sent me.[41] He that receiveth a prophet in the name of a prophet shall receive a prophet's reward; and he that receiveth a righteous man in the name of a righteous man shall receive a righteous man's reward.[42] And whosoever shall give to drink unto one of these little ones a cup of cold water only in the name of a disciple, verily I say unto you, he shall in no wise lose his reward.

In summary, we find four dangers for the believer experiencing persecution as outlined in this section of Matthew 10. They include the following:

- denying Christ,
- loving family more than Christ,
- loving one's own life more than Christ, and
- refusing to receive those who were wanted by authorities or mobs because of their witness for Jesus Christ.

The cross was an instrument of execution. It was used by the state for the worst types of criminals. Every criminal to be crucified had to carry his own cross. Jesus died on the cross to atone for our sins. We cannot do that. And the cross is not simply self-denial or dying to self or giving everything to self. There is an element of persecution in it. We must be willing to pay any cost to see the will of God accomplished, even to our own death. Jesus is calling us to martyrdom if necessary. Josef Ton has been quoted repeatedly (though a friend provided the terms) "His cross is for propitiation; ours is for propagation."[12] Our death witnesses to the truth of Christ's death for us and love for us. It is important to remember that martyrdom is not the same as a suicide bomber. He dies to kill; the martyr dies to give life. He chooses to die; the true martyr is willing to die if necessary, but the path is chosen for him.

Jesus said: *Mt. 16:[18] And I say also unto thee, that thou art Peter, and upon this rock I will build my church; and the gates of hell shall not prevail against it.* Jesus is building His church. He will work in such a way that Satan cannot stop or defeat it. Jesus initiates the church through the cross. But His message will not reach the entire world without the self-sacrifice of the messenger.

Once again, we note that Jesus spoke about persecution in Matthew 16:21-28 immediately after Peter's confession that Jesus is not only the Messiah but the Son of the living God. *Matthew 16:[21] From that time forth began Jesus to show unto his disciples, how that he must go unto Jerusalem, and suffer many things are the elders and chief priests and scribes, and be killed, and be raised again the third day. [22] Then Peter took him, and began to rebuke him, saying, Be it far from thee, Lord, that shall not be unto thee. [23] But he turned; and said unto Peter, Get the behind me Satan: thou art an offense unto me: for thou savourest not the things that be of God, but those that be of men. [24] Then said Jesus unto his disciples, If any man would will come after me, let him deny himself, and take up his cross, and follow me. [25] For whosoever will save his life shall lose it: and whosoever will lose his life for my sake shall find it. [26] For what is a man profited, if he shall gain the whole world, and lose his own soul? Or what shall a man give in exchange for soul? [27] For the Son of man shall come in the glory of his Father with his angels; and then he shall reward every man according to his works. [28] Verily I say unto you, there shall be some standing here which shall not taste of death, till they see the Son of Man coming in his kingdom.*

Peter had realized that Jesus was the Messiah. In his mind, the Messiah would be victorious, but resulting from a manner which man is accustomed to use; power, and if necessary, violence. In his concern for Jesus, he expressed the same philosophy that Satan had used in the temptation in the wilderness. The idea was: Save yourself. Avoid the cross. Compromise. Actually, the priests at Jesus' crucifixion spoke more truth than they realized, when they said: *Mt. 27:[41] Likewise also the chief priests mocking him, with the scribes and elders, said,[42] He saved others; himself he cannot save. If he be the King of Israel, let him now come down from the cross, and we will believe him. Indeed, if Jesus were to save us, then He could not save Himself.*

Likewise, we must be prepared to face possible death when we are following our Master, Jesus Christ. Crucifixion itself is a terrible punishment. Crucifixion was a state punishment reserved for the worst sort of criminals. As Christ's death was the foundation of the church, our deaths may be necessary to build his church. We are to be witnesses. There are great rewards resulting from faithfulness to him. These rewards are given to those who will receive His grace and sufficiency, not just renounce the world for the sake of reward. We show ourselves worthy of God's trust as we serve Him and obey Him here in the world. The trials and tribulations here on earth are in preparation to train us for our tasks in heaven. Our rewards will be to serve and rule with Him for eternity.

Martyrdom happens *to* you, not *by* you. Therefore, a suicide bomber is not really a martyr. We need this training through persecution for the tasks which we will have in eternity. When we accept His grace, it is both saving and enabling grace. Thus, we need to avoid two errors. We need to know that we do not earn God's favor through our own efforts or living sacrificially to gain reward. Also, we do not gain God's favor through the pursuit of self-scrutiny and self-discipline. The focus instead is on Christ and His purposes.

The true disciple is only doing his duty and is thankful for God's grace. *Luke 17:[7] But which of you, having a servant plowing or feeding cattle, will say unto him by and by, when he is come from the field, Go and sit down to meat? [8] And will not rather send him, make ready wherewith I may sup, and gird thyself and serve me, till I have eaten and drunken, and afterward thou shalt eat and drink? [9] Doth he thank that servant because he did the things which are commanded of him? I trow not. [10] So likewise ye, when ye shall have done all these things which are commanded you, say, We are unprofitable servants: we have done that which was our duty to do.*

Persecution in the Gospel of Mark

The book of Mark was probably the first gospel written. We find a key to persecution in *Mark 8:[34] And when he had called the people unto him with his disciples also, he said unto them, Whosoever will come after me, let him deny himself, and take up his cross, and follow me.[35] For whosoever will save his life shall lose it; but whosoever shall lose his life for my sake and the gospel's, the same shall save it.[36] For what shall it profit a man, if he shall gain the whole world, and lose his own soul?[37] Or what shall a man give in exchange for his soul?* The cross was the only path to Jesus' glory, and the cross is the path for the glory for His disciples. They do not seek ambition or power, but seek to serve, especially those in misery and need. Often the disciples failed to understand, argued for position, and eventually denied Jesus or ran away. But Jesus did not leave them, and after His resurrection they served Him until their deaths as martyrs. Yet how do people respond to persecution? Some believe. Some are afraid and say nothing. Some leave Christian fellowship completely. That was true in the time of Christ, and it is true today.

Persecution in the Gospel of Luke

Persecution is more than rejection of the person; it is the rejection of God's agents. Simeon mentioned this to Mary in Luke Chapter 2. In the gospel of Luke, we find persecution is expected of God's people. Simeon predicts persecution to Mary in *Luke 2:[34] And Simeon blessed them, and said unto Mary his mother, Behold, this child is set for the fall and rising again of many in Israel; and for a sign which shall be spoken against;* Notice that the sign will be opposed. The Scriptures have said that the servant-Messiah must die.

The supposed people of God often misused and persecuted the prophets. It is the false prophets who were well spoken of, but the persecuted believers stand in continuity with the Old

Testament prophets. Persecution is in the plan of God. *Luke 6:[22] Blessed are ye, when men shall hate you, and when they shall separate you from their company, and shall reproach you, and cast out your name as evil, for the Son of man's sake.[23] Rejoice ye in that day, and leap for joy: for, behold, your reward is great in heaven: for in the like manner did their fathers unto the prophets.[24] But woe unto you that are rich! for ye have received your consolation.[25] Woe unto you that are full! for ye shall hunger. Woe unto you that laugh now! for ye shall mourn and weep.[26] Woe unto you, when all men shall speak well of you! for so did their fathers to the false prophets.* Thus, the disciples can anticipate being persecuted like Jesus.

There are several themes of persecution in Luke. First, persecution was in the plan of God. We find the first clues from Simeon early in Luke. Luke concludes with the same theme: *Lk. 24:[44] And he said unto them, These are the words which I spake unto you, while I was yet with you, that all things must be fulfilled, which were written in the law of Moses, and in the prophets, and in the psalms, concerning me.[45] Then opened he their understanding, that they might understand the scriptures, [46] And said unto them, Thus it is written, and thus it behooved Christ to suffer, and to rise from the dead the third day:[47] And that repentance and remission of sins should be preached in his name among all nations, beginning at Jerusalem.[48] And ye are witnesses of these things.*

Luke shows that this persecution was in the plan of God from the beginning. Thus, the scriptures were fulfilled. And if Jesus' persecution and death was part of God's plan, then the death of His disciples was also part of God's plan.

Second, persecution is the rejection of God's agents. We have already seen that the prophets were rejected, usually by the very people they came to serve. Jesus was rejected, as prophesied by Simeon, and began in Luke 4 with His rejection in his own hometown, where they tried to kill Him. *Lk. 4:[22] And all bare him witness and wondered at the gracious words which proceeded out of his mouth. And they said, Is not this Joseph's son?[23] And he said unto them, Ye will surely say unto me this proverb, Physician, heal thyself: whatsoever we have heard done in Capernaum, do also here in thy country.[24] And he said, Verily I say unto you, No prophet is accepted in his own country.* Their rejection led to His crucifixion. The disciples who will carry on His ministry will also be rejected.

Third, persecution is an integral consequence of following Jesus. *Luke 6:[22] Blessed are ye, when men shall hate you, and when they shall separate you from their company, and shall reproach you, and cast out your name as evil, for the Son of man's sake. Luke 21:[12] But before all these, they shall lay their hands on you, and persecute you, delivering you up to the synagogues, and into prisons, being brought before kings and rulers for my name's sake.[13] And it shall turn to you for a testimony...[16] And ye shall be betrayed both by parents, and brethren, and kinsfolks, and friends; and some of you shall they cause to be put to death.[17] And ye shall be hated of all men for my name's sake.*

Discipleship is linked with the cross. *Luke 9:[22] Saying, The Son of man must suffer many things, and be rejected of the elders and chief priests and scribes, and be slain, and be raised the third day.[23] And he said to them all, If any man will come after me, let him deny himself, and take up his cross daily, and follow me.[24] For whosoever will save his life shall lose it: but whosoever will lose his life for my sake, the same shall save it.[25] For what is a man advantaged, if he gain the whole world, and lose himself, or be cast away? Every day the disciple should make a commitment that His will be first in his life. Luke 14:[27] And whosoever doth not bear his cross, and come after me, cannot be my disciple.* We must count the cost and be prepared to pay it if we wish to be His disciples.

But persecution is the time of divine triumph. The fate of the disciples is actually in God's hands. God can deliver from physical harm, or God can give the ultimate delivery from evil.

And God promises to give the right words for effective witness. *Luke 12:[11] And when they bring you unto the synagogues, and unto magistrates, and powers, take ye no thought how or what thing ye shall answer, or what ye shall say:[12] For the Holy Ghost shall teach you in the same hour what ye ought to say. Luke 21:[12] But before all these, they shall lay their hands on you, and persecute you, delivering you up to the synagogues, and into prisons, being brought before kings and rulers for my name's sake.[13] And it shall turn to you for a testimony. [14] Settle it therefore in your hearts, not to meditate before what ye shall answer: [15] For I will give you a mouth and wisdom, which all your adversaries shall not be able to gainsay nor resist.*

Persecution is a time for Christian perseverance. We must remain loyal to Christ. Will we deny Christ or acknowledge Him before men? Peter is an example of how not to persevere. After affirming that he would never deny Christ, he did so three times. But Jesus, who is full of compassion, later restored him.

Persecution is an integral consequence of following Jesus. He was hated because He was the Son of Man. Jesus warned that we will be hated by all for His sake. Persecution is the occasion for Christian perseverance. It is a time of testing. *Luke 10:[19] Behold, I give unto you power to tread on serpents and scorpions, and over all the power of the enemy; and nothing shall by any means hurt you; [20] Notwithstanding in this rejoice not, that the spirits are subject unto you, but rather rejoice, because your names are written in heaven. Luke 21:[17] And ye shall be hated of all men for my name's sake. [18] But there shall not an hair of your head perish.*

There is an additional thought from the parable Jesus spoke in *Luke 19:[11] And as they heard these things, he added and spake a parable, because he was nigh to Jerusalem, and because they thought that the kingdom of God should immediately appear.[12] He said therefore, A certain nobleman went into a far country to receive for himself a kingdom, and to return.[13] And he called his ten servants, and delivered them ten pounds, and said unto them, Occupy till I come.[14] But his citizens hated him, and sent a message after him, saying, We will not have this man to reign over us.[15] And it came to pass, that when he was returned, having received the kingdom, then he commanded these servants to be called unto him, to whom he had given the money, that he might know how much every man had gained by trading.[16] Then came the first, saying, Lord, thy pound hath gained ten pounds.[17] And he said unto him, Well, thou good servant: because thou hast been faithful in a very little, have thou authority over ten cities.[18] And the second came, saying, Lord, thy pound hath gained five pounds.[19] And he said likewise to him, Be thou also over five cities. [20] And another came, saying, Lord, behold, here is thy pound, which I have kept laid up in a napkin:[21] For I feared thee, because thou art an austere man: thou takest up that thou layedst not down, and reapest that thou didst not sow.[22] And he saith unto him, Out of thine own mouth will I judge thee, thou wicked servant. Thou knewest that I was an austere man, taking up that I laid not down, and reaping that I did not sow:[23] Wherefore then gavest not thou my money into the bank, that at my coming I might have required mine own with usury?[24] And he said unto them that stood by, Take from him the pound, and give it to him that hath ten pounds.[25] (And they said unto him, Lord, he hath ten pounds.)[26] For I say unto you, That unto every one which hath shall be given; and from him that hath not, even that he hath shall be taken away from him.[27] But those mine enemies, which would not that I should reign over them, bring hither, and slay them before me.*

The context is clear. Jesus is approaching Jerusalem and the disciples expect that He will take over as Messiah. He shows them that this is not true, and that He will go but return later. (Apparently there is a historical event that also fits with this situation.) The important fact I would like to emphasize is that the work here on earth has direct bearing on the reward in heaven. Those who work hard for Christ here will have great rewards in heaven. They have shown themselves worthy during testing here on earth. On earth, we are simply stewards, and nothing is truly ours. We brought nothing at birth, and we can take nothing (materially) at death. But we do develop character and show our loyalty to Christ.

Jesus gives us another illustration in the parable of the unrighteous steward. *Luke 16:[1] And he said also unto his disciples, There was a certain rich man, which had a steward; and the same was accused unto him that he had wasted his goods.[2] And he called him, and said unto him, How is it that I hear this of thee? give an account of thy stewardship; for thou mayest be no longer steward.[3] Then the steward said within himself, What shall I do? for my lord taketh away from me the stewardship: I cannot dig; to beg I am ashamed.[4] I am resolved what to do, that, when I am put out of the stewardship, they may receive me into their houses.[5] So he called every one of his lord's debtors unto him, and said unto the first, How much owest thou unto my lord?[6] And he said, An hundred measures of oil. And he said unto him, Take thy bill, and sit down quickly, and write fifty.[7] Then said he to another, And how much owest thou? And he said, An hundred measures of wheat. And he said unto him, Take thy bill, and write fourscore. [8] And the lord commended the unjust steward, because he had done wisely: for the children of this world are in their generation wiser than the children of light.[9] And I say unto you, Make to yourselves friends of the mammon of unrighteousness; that, when ye fail, they may receive you into everlasting habitations.[10] He that is faithful in that which is least is faithful also in much: and he that is unjust in the least is unjust also in much.[11] If therefore ye have not been faithful in the unrighteous mammon, who will commit to your trust the true riches?[12] And if ye have not been faithful in that which is another man's, who shall give you that which is your own?[13] No servant can serve two masters: for either he will hate the one, and love the other; or else he will hold to the one, and despise the other. Ye cannot serve God and mammon.*

Why did Jesus commend the unrighteous steward? He certainly did not commend him as a thief, but the steward was wise in providing for his future. We also should be wise in providing for our future. The steward used his position, although temporary now, to establish a better future. The same way, we should use the "unrighteous mammon" of material goods now to serve our Lord so that we will have rewards in heaven. Jesus encourages this also in the sermon on the mount. *Mt. 6:[19] Lay not up for yourselves treasures upon earth, where moth and rust doth corrupt, and where thieves break through and steal:[20] But lay up for yourselves treasures in heaven, where neither moth nor rust doth corrupt, and where thieves do not break through nor steal:[21] For where your treasure is, there will your heart be also.*

It also appears that the character we develop on earth will somehow be transmitted to heaven. Here on earth, we are being trained and our character is being developed, but we are also being tested for our loyalty and reliability.[13] If we are not reliable here, God will not entrust the true riches of heaven to us. Riches on earth are temporary. They are not really our own. Responsibilities in heaven are forever and are truly ours. Look again at verse 12. God wants to put us, as His sons, in charge of our inheritance. We are co-inheritors with Christ, who is ruler over everything. But He will not place us as rulers if we are not trustworthy and faithful.

Persecution in the Gospel of John

In the gospel of John, Jesus reveals that He is the only source of life. Mankind is divided into those who accepted Him and those who did not. *John 1:[10] He was in the world, and the world was made by him, and the world knew him not.[11] He came unto his own, and his own received him not.[12] But as many as received him, to them gave he power to become the sons of God, even to them that believe on his name.*

Some of those who appeared to accept Him at first did not

persist in following Him. *Jn. 2:[23] Now when he was in Jerusalem at the passover, in the feast day, many believed in his name, when they saw the miracles which he did.[24] But Jesus did not commit himself unto them, because he knew all men,[25] And needed not that any should testify of man: for he knew what was in man.*

This fickle attitude became clear after His discourse on the bread of life. *Jn. 6:[60] Many therefore of his disciples, when they had heard this, said, This is an hard saying; who can hear it?[61] When Jesus knew in himself that his disciples murmured at it, he said unto them, Doth this offend you?[62] What and if ye shall see the Son of man ascend up where he was before?[63] It is the spirit that quickeneth; the flesh profiteth nothing: the words that I speak unto you, they are spirit, and they are life.[64] But there are some of you that believe not. For Jesus knew from the beginning who they were that believed not, and who should betray him.[65] And he said, Therefore said I unto you, that no man can come unto me, except it were given unto him of my Father.[66] From that time many of his disciples went back, and walked no more with him.* We must remain faithful. He must be central in our lives.

There was great hatred for Jesus. His own family rejected him. He was threatened with arrest. He was threatened with stoning. His reputation was spoiled. He was slandered. He was arrested and killed. Jesus laid down His life for us. His disciples will experience the same while sharing the gospel. On the night of His betrayal, Jesus warned them of coming persecution. *Jn. 15:[18] If the world hate you, ye know that it hated me before it hated you.[19] If ye were of the world, the world would love his own: but because ye are not of the world, but I have chosen you out of the world, therefore the world hateth you.[20] Remember the word that I said unto you, The servant is not greater than his lord. If they have persecuted me, they will also persecute you; if they have kept my saying, they will keep yours also.[21] But all these things will they do unto you for my name's sake, because they know not him that sent me.*

He goes further in *Jn. 16:[1] These things have I spoken unto you, that ye should not be offended.[2] They shall put you out of the synagogues: yea, the time cometh, that whosoever killeth you will think that he doeth God service.[3] And these things will they do unto you, because they have not known the Father, nor me.[4] But these things have I told you, that when the time shall come, ye may remember that I told you of them. And these things I said not unto you at the beginning, because I was with you.*

Penner makes a startling observation:

> *"The believers are to remain in a relationship of love and trust in the face of the unbelief and hatred of the world. Persecution cannot and will not be stopped by persuasion, education, or legislation. The world does these things simply because they do not know God. The world's hatred is not ultimately rooted in hatred of Christians; it is rooted in hatred toward God."* [14]

We need to remember the world did not come to Jesus through signs and wonders which He performed, but when He was lifted up on the cross. *John 12:[32] And I, if I be lifted up from the earth, will draw all men unto me. [33] This he said, signifying what death he should die.* Thus, fruitfulness comes through dying. This is a call to martyrdom. *Jn. 12:[23] And Jesus answered them, saying, The hour is come, that the Son of man should be glorified.[24] Verily, verily, I say unto you, Except a corn of wheat fall into the ground and die, it abideth alone: but if it die, it bringeth forth much fruit.[25] He that loveth his life shall lose it; and he that hateth his life in this world shall keep it unto life eternal.[26] If any man serve me, let him follow me; and where I am, there shall also my servant be: if any man serve me, him will my Father honour.* Jesus uses another example here — the seed. A seed has to "die" in the ground before it can give much fruit. Fruitfulness requires dying.[15]

Jesus speaks a great deal about the coming Comforter and abiding in Him during his lengthy discussion in John 13-17. Without Him we can do nothing. We must abide in Him. We must remember that the Holy Spirit is not only the Comforter to strengthen us in trials and persecutions which are to come, but He also is a witness. *Jn. 16:[8] And when he is come, he will reprove the world of sin, and of righteousness, and of judgment:[9] Of sin, because they believe not on me;[10] Of righteousness, because I go to my Father, and ye see me no more;[11] Of judgment, because the prince of this world is judged.* The Holy Spirit witnesses of Christ.

Jesus goes on to say: *Jn. 16:[12] I have yet many things to say unto you, but ye cannot bear them now.[13] Howbeit when he, the Spirit of truth, is come, he will guide you into all truth: for he shall not speak of himself; but whatsoever he shall hear, that shall he speak: and he will shew you things to come.[14] He shall glorify me: for he shall receive of mine, and shall shew it unto you.[15] All things that the Father hath are mine: therefore said I, that he shall take of mine, and shall shew it unto you.* He will comfort us, strengthen us, and enable our witness for Christ.

Persecution in the Book of Acts

As we read the book of Acts, we find that the disciples are ambassadors of Jesus Christ. They have His power and authority. Everything they achieve will be His achievement through His Holy Spirit. We also learn that The Holy Spirit is the Comforter during persecution and that persecution offers more opportunities to witness. When the disciples fled, they did not go underground, but witnessed in a public manner. Opposition inevitably followed the preaching of the gospel.

The book of Acts is an extension of Luke's gospel, and after the resurrection, Jesus gives an indication of what is to come as He walks toward Emmaus with two disciples. They were downcast from the death of Christ. *Luke 24:[25] Then he said unto them, O fools, and slow of heart to believe all that the prophets have spoken:[26] Ought not Christ to have suffered these things, and to enter into his glory?[27] And beginning at Moses and all the prophets, he expounded unto them in all the scriptures the things concerning himself.* Thus, first Christ will suffer, and then He will be glorified.

After He revealed Himself to them and disappeared, they returned to the disciples, where Jesus appeared in their midst. *Luke 24:[44] And he said unto them, These are the words which I spake unto you, while I was yet with you, that all things must be fulfilled, which were written in the law of Moses, and in the prophets, and in the psalms, concerning me.[45] Then opened he their understanding, that they might understand the scriptures,[46] And said unto them, Thus it is written, and thus it behooved Christ to suffer, and to rise from the dead the third day:[47] And that repentance and remission of sins should be preached in his name among all nations, beginning at Jerusalem.[48] And ye are witnesses of these things.* This same message must be spread to all nations by His disciples.

The disciples were to remain in Jerusalem until the Holy Spirit arrived, who was necessary for their effective witness. *Acts 1:[8] But ye shall receive power, after that the Holy Ghost is come upon you: and ye shall be witnesses unto me both in Jerusalem, and in all Judaea, and in Samaria, and unto the uttermost part of the earth.* Jerusalem was a dangerous place for them to be, but in obedience to the Lord, they stayed there despite beatings, imprisonment, and eventually martyrdom.

Ton makes the following observations: The implications of this promise are enormous. First of all, it tells the disciples that they will not be alone in the battle; the Holy Spirit will be both in them and with them. Secondly, it makes them aware that this battle is actually not their own; it is God's initiative and God's action and concern. They are His ambassadors, fully endowed with His authority and power. Thirdly, whatever they will achieve will be God's achievement, because God's Spirit has worked in them.[16]

Throughout the book of Acts, we see persecution of Peter, John, Paul and others. We find two martyrs die, and observe whipping, being jailed, stoned, and chased out of town. Yet as you look at the results of the persecution, the gospel spread. Persecution provided more opportunities to witness. When the disciples fled, they did not go "underground" and hide. Their witness was public; they continued to preach. Opposition inevitably followed the gospel. Church growth and the spread of the gospel tended to cause persecution. Religious and church leaders rose up to stop the movement. Persecution came from a variety of sources and for a variety of reasons. We find the same reasons persist until today. When witness is minimal, persecution is minimal, but when witnessing is followed by many coming to Christ, persecution from unbelievers can be expected.

We find these events in the first church occurred as it had explosive growth. Church growth and the spread of the Gospel often results in persecution, but persecution can also lead to explosive growth. This was especially noted after the death of the first martyr, Stephen. *Acts 8:[1] And Saul was consenting unto his death. And at that time there was a great persecution against the church which was at Jerusalem; and they were all scattered abroad throughout the regions of Judaea and Samaria, except the apostles.[2] And devout men carried Stephen to his burial, and made great lamentation over him.[3] As for Saul, he made havock of the church, entering into every house, and haling men and women committed them to prison.[4] Therefore they that were scattered abroad went everywhere preaching the word.*

Persecution came from a variety of sources and ways. Why was there persecution? There was religious persecution because the Christian religion was a threat to the existing system of Jewish religion. The Christian faith spoke of a personal relationship with a personal redeemer, Jesus Christ. The official leaders had rejected Him as a deceiver.

There were political reasons, because the Christian's primary loyalty was to Christ and not to the nation. The Romans demanded a certain level of loyalty from their citizens. They were to accept the Caesar as one of their gods, and indeed the divine head of their religion. There was an exception made for Jews, and as long as Christians were considered a Jewish sect, the Romans tolerated them. But when it became clear that Christianity was a separate religion, and that indeed the official Jewish leaders repudiated them, then persecution occurred beginning with the rule of Nero.

There were social reasons, because sometimes Christianity would break the societal and family norms. Loyalty to Christ was above loyalty to family. There were economic reasons, because Christianity interfered with particular businesses. This was especially true of the idolatry associated with making idols of the Temple of Diana. And there was much jealousy by the religious leaders leading to emotional causes for persecution. When large crowds began to listen to Paul in the Jewish synagogues, the Jewish leaders reacted with persecution in such places as Antioch (Acts 13:45 ff) and Thessalonica (Acts 16:4 ff).

However, persecution was part of the plan of God. When the Jews killed Stephen, they thought that they were serving God. God permitted that persecution, which then spread the church widely into new areas. Paul spoke before kings and governors expecting persecution. *Acts 20:[22] And now, behold, I go bound in the spirit unto Jerusalem, not knowing the things that shall befall me there:[23] Save that the Holy Ghost witnesseth in every city, saying that bonds and afflictions abide me.[24] But none of these things move me, neither count I my life dear unto myself, so that I might finish my course with joy, and the ministry, which I have received of the Lord Jesus, to testify the gospel of the grace of God. He was bound, but the word was not bound. 2 Tim. 2:[9] Wherein I suffer trouble, as an evil doer, even unto bonds; but the word of God is not bound.*

Persecution, especially by the religious leaders, was, in reality, the rejection of God's agents. The result of Stephen's preaching was exactly what happened to the prophets. Stephen preached that the Jewish leaders were always persecuting God's prophets. When the Sanhedrin killed Stephen, they simply confirmed his message. Thus, the persecuted stand in line with God's prophets of the Old Testament. Persecution is an integral consequence of following the Lord Jesus Christ and claiming Him as the risen Lord.

The apostles were often declared innocent by Roman authorities. They were not apostate Jews rejecting what the Jewish prophets had proclaimed. But they proclaimed that Jesus is Lord, and the world would not tolerate that message. However, persecution is also the occasion of divine triumph. The church grows despite persecution. Sometimes the gospel is spread because of persecution. God's victory is His ability to keep the disciples faithful in the midst of affliction. They remain obedient even when the situation itself does not change.

Why would disciples be ready to suffer and die? They knew that God was sovereign. The term they used (despota) means absolute sovereign authority. Their work was to witness boldly in the power of the Holy Spirit. They prayed for boldness to preach, and for signs and wonders to lift up the name of the Lord Jesus. After Peter and John were admonished by the Sanhedrin, the ruling authority of the Jews, they rejoiced as they joined the other believers. The believers prayed for boldness and effective witness. Their prayer began by quoting Psalm 2.

Acts 4:[26] The kings of the earth stood up, and the rulers were gathered together against the Lord, and against his Christ.[27] For of a truth against thy holy child Jesus, whom thou hast anointed, both Herod, and Pontius Pilate, with the Gentiles, and the people of Israel, were gathered together,[28] For to do whatsoever thy hand and thy counsel determined before to be done.[29] And now, Lord, behold their threatenings: and grant unto thy servants, that with all boldness they may speak thy word,[30] By stretching forth thine hand to heal; and that signs and wonders may be done by the name of thy holy child Jesus.[31] And when they had prayed, the place was shaken where they were assembled together; and they were all filled with the Holy Ghost, and they spake the word of God with boldness.

They viewed suffering for Christ as a privilege and an honor. *Acts 5:[40] And to him they agreed: and when they had called the apostles, and beaten them, they commanded that they should not speak in the name of Jesus and let them go. [41] And they departed from the presence of the council, rejoicing that they were counted worthy to suffer shame for his name. [42] And daily in the temple, and in every house, they ceased not to teach and preach Jesus Christ.* They rejoiced that they were counted worthy to suffer for His name.

They had a clear perception of the glory of martyrdom. In Luke's gospel and in Acts, Luke drew many parallels between Stephen and Jesus in their trials and deaths as martyrs. Stephen was not a passive recipient of punishment. Stephen himself was the aggressor, witnessing, forgiving, testifying, and entrusting his spirit to God.

As we summarize the lessons of the book of Acts, the first lesson is that God is sovereign. Everything that occurred to the apostles and others was orchestrated and permitted by God Himself. They were not ultimately defeated but were victors, not victims. Second, it was an honor to be selected to be persecuted and abused for Christ. *Acts 5:[41] And they departed from the presence of the council, rejoicing that they were counted worthy to suffer shame for his name.*

Paul and Silas were able to rejoice in their suffering in prison. And Paul was able to come back into Lystra after being stoned to encourage the saints to keep on and look to the future rewards. *Acts 14:[22] Confirming the souls of the disciples, and exhorting them to continue in the faith, and that we must through much tribulation enter into the kingdom of God.* They had a clear vision of the blessings of martyrdom.

Jozef Ton explains further about the vision which Stephen

65

saw as he was dying as a martyr.[17] The first benefit is that of a witness. In Stephen's case, if truly Jesus was standing in heaven at the Father's right hand, then the Sanhedrin was terribly wrong in condemning Him to death. This they would not accept, and they killed the messenger. Secondly, it is a tremendous encouragement to the person who is then being tortured or facing death. Thirdly, the prayer of forgiveness shows those who are witnessing the persecution the true love which God alone can give. Finally, the Holy Spirit empowers the witness.

Suffering in the Pauline Epistles

Paul experienced suffering almost immediately after his conversion. Although this might be expected in his case because he had previously persecuted believers and now "switched sides," many new believers also suffered persecution. It is important that they be prepared for this fact. Paul knew much about suffering. When God called Ananias to go to Paul, He told him: *"for I will show him how great things they must suffer for my name's sake: Acts 9:16.* In *1 Thessalonians 1:[6] And ye became followers of us, and of the Lord, having received the word in much affliction, with joy of the Holy Ghost:* Paul demonstrates that they are followers of him also in his sufferings. Paul was pleased and relieved to find that they were persisting despite their sufferings and persecution. He had warned them that this was part of being a Christian.

When Paul could no longer go back to Thessalonica because of the rulers taking a bond from Jason to prevent his return, he wanted to know how things went with them in their persecution. In 2 Thessalonians, we find that our suffering may persist throughout life, but eventually it will stop. *2 Thessalonians 1:[4] So that we ourselves glory in you in the churches of God for your patience and faith in all your persecutions and tribulations that ye endure:[5] Which is a manifest token of the righteous judgment of God, that ye may be counted worthy of the kingdom of God, for which ye also suffer:[6] Seeing it is a righteous thing with God to recompense tribulation to them that trouble you;[7]*

And to you who are troubled rest with us, when the Lord Jesus shall be revealed from heaven with his mighty angels,[8] In flaming fire taking vengeance on them that know not God, and that obey not the gospel of our Lord Jesus Christ:[9] Who shall be punished with everlasting destruction from the presence of the Lord, and from the glory of his power;[10] When he shall come to be glorified in his saints, and to be admired in all them that believe (because our testimony among you was believed) in that day. Suffering with faith and patience shows worthiness of the kingdom of God. It also demonstrates that God is righteous in punishing the oppressors. God's repayment shall and will last throughout eternity.

As Paul anticipated the coming of the Lord, his concern for believers was whether or not they would prove themselves worthy of the kingdom of God. Suffering may last throughout life, but then it will stop. Thus, it is not *if* we suffer or *why* we suffer, but *how* we suffer that is key. Will we allow suffering to prepare us for eternity? Or will we insist on the rewards of eternity now, and then receive nothing further then? We must pray that our work is *His work* and we are manifestations of *His life* to the world. **Only what is done in His power will last for eternity**. Paul prays that his own work will be done by God's power, and that God will protect him from evil men, who will inevitably oppose his message.

Persecution in First and Second Corinthians

Paul reveals much about persecution in 1 Corinthians. *1 Corinthians 1:[17] For Christ sent me not to baptize, but to preach the gospel: not with wisdom of words, lest the cross of Christ should be made of none effect.[18] For the preaching of the cross is to them that perish foolishness; but unto us which are saved it is the power of God.[19] For it is written, I will destroy the wisdom of the wise, and will bring to nothing the understanding of the prudent.[20] Where is the wise? Where is the scribe? Where is the disputer of this world? hath not God made foolish the wisdom of this world?[21] For after that in the*

67

wisdom of God the world by wisdom knew not God, it pleased God by the foolishness of preaching to save them that believe.[22] For the Jews require a sign, and the Greeks seek after wisdom:[23] But we preach Christ crucified, unto the Jews a stumbling block, and unto the Greeks foolishness;[24] But unto them which are called, both Jews and Greeks, Christ the power of God, and the wisdom of God. [25] Because the foolishness of God is wiser than men; and the weakness of God is stronger than men.[26] For ye see your calling, brethren, how that not many wise men after the flesh, not many mighty, not many noble, are called:[27] But God hath chosen the foolish things of the world to confound the wise; and God hath chosen the weak things of the world to confound the things which are mighty;[28] And base things of the world, and things which are despised, hath God chosen, yea, and things which are not, to bring to nought things that are:[29] That no flesh should glory in his presence.[30] But of him are ye in Christ Jesus, who of God is made unto us wisdom, and righteousness, and sanctification, and redemption:[31] That, according as it is written, He that glorieth, let him glory in the Lord.

God's methods are different from man's methods. Man's methods, the way of the world, use the wisdom and power of the world. Man uses the rich, the wise, and the powerful, but God uses the base and simple things of the world to accomplish His purposes. This is shown in Christ (we will see this more completely in Philippians 2:5-11), and it is Christ in us who accomplishes God's will. This brings great glory to God.

Paul goes on to show that this is his method of ministry so that we will trust in God, and not in ourselves. Paul depends on the Holy Spirit to work in the lives of the listeners to accomplish a change in heart that is permanent. Only the Holy Spirit can convince the listener that Jesus Christ, who was condemned by His own people and the Roman government, and who was permitted to be condemned by God Himself, is actually the source of salvation.

This is the mission of any messenger of Christ. First, we must demonstrate His incarnation in our lives, rather than serving self. Second, we must bear the cross, rather than focus on self-preservation. In weakness and dependency on God, we show God's grace, rather than our own stability and strength. Paul deliberately ministered in weakness and foolishness. Thus, he demonstrated the power of the Spirit rather than his own capability.

When we fail to pick up our cross to follow Christ, we are really abandoning Him. The message of the cross will be rejected by the world. It will be accepted only by the work of the Holy Spirit. Our preaching will fail without the demonstration of the Spirit working in our lives, and our reliance on Him to move in the hearts of the hearers. There is a danger entrusting ourselves as communicators in our own ability. The difference of the power of the Spirit is seen both in the message and in the messenger.

1 Corinthians 2:[1] And I, brethren, when I came to you, came not with excellency of speech or of wisdom, declaring unto you the testimony of God.[2] For I determined not to know anything among you, save Jesus Christ, and him crucified.[3] And I was with you in weakness, and in fear, and in much trembling.[4] And my speech and my preaching was not with enticing words of man's wisdom, but in demonstration of the Spirit and of power:[5] That your faith should not stand in the wisdom of men, but in the power of God.

God's messengers work through God's methods. *1 Corinthians 1:[9] God is faithful, by whom ye were called unto the fellowship of his Son Jesus Christ our Lord.* This is how His messengers work: *1 Cor. 4:[9] For I think that God hath set forth us the apostles last, as it were appointed to death: for we are made a spectacle unto the world, and to angels, and to men.[10] We are fools for Christ's sake, but ye are wise in Christ; we are weak, but ye are strong; ye are honourable, but we are despised.[11] Even unto this present hour we both hunger, and thirst, and are naked, and are buffeted, and have no certain dwelling place;[12] And labour, working with our own hands: being reviled, we bless; being persecuted, we suffer it:[13] Being defamed, we intreat: we are made as the filth of the world, and are the offscouring of all things unto this day.* Thus, the service of God is incarnational, serving others; characterized by the cross; and working through weakness rather than strength.

Let us consider the rewards briefly mentioned in *1 Corinthians 3:[9] For we are labourers together with God: ye are God's husbandry, ye are God's building.[10] According to the grace of God which is given unto me, as a wise master builder, I have laid the foundation, and another buildeth thereon. But let every man take heed how he buildeth thereupon.[11] For other foundation can no man lay than that is laid, which is Jesus Christ.[12] Now if any man build upon this foundation gold, silver, precious stones, wood, hay, stubble;[13] Every man's work shall be made manifest: for the day shall declare it, because it shall be revealed by fire; and the fire shall try every man's work of what sort it is.[14] If any man's work abide which he hath built thereupon, he shall receive a reward.[15] If any man's work shall be burned, he shall suffer loss: but he himself shall be saved; yet so as by fire.*

The emphasis here seems to be on the *quality* of work rather than the *quantity* of work. The works will be tested by fire, and this certainly fits with persecution. Those who pass the test are rewarded. The others are not lost sinners going to hell but saved individuals who have lost much of their potential reward.

Jozef Ton, whom I have quoted often, is concerned with the question of rewards in heaven. I believe that he is correct that there are rewards in heaven, and that people who live differently will receive different rewards in heaven. The word inheritance is important, as we shall see. *1 Corinthians 6:[9] Know ye not that the unrighteous shall not inherit the kingdom of God? Be not deceived: neither fornicators, nor idolaters, nor adulterers, nor effeminate, nor abusers of themselves with mankind,[10] Nor thieves, nor covetous, nor drunkards, nor revilers, nor extortioners, shall inherit the kingdom of God.[11] And such were some of you: but ye are washed, but ye are sanctified, but ye are justified in the name of the Lord Jesus, and by the Spirit of our God.*

I struggled with these verses. Does this mean that someone who appears genuinely saved but struggling with drugs or alcohol is condemned to hell? Absolutely not. It is quite possible to be a son and yet not have the inheritance which the father intended if you prove unworthy. We will see this theme developed more as we proceed.

Likewise, Paul states that if there were no rewards in the future, we Christians are to be pitied. *1 Cor. 15:[19] If in this life only we have hope in Christ, we are of all men most miserable.* He goes on to explain that we suffer with the hope of future rewards in heaven. *1 Cor. 15:[29] Else what shall they do which are baptized for the dead, if the dead rise not at all? why are they then baptized for the dead?[30] And why stand we in jeopardy every hour?[31] I protest by your rejoicing which I have in Christ Jesus our Lord, I die daily.[32] If after the manner of men I have fought with beasts at Ephesus, what advantageth it me, if the dead rise not? let us eat and drink; for tomorrow we die.*

I believe that the term baptism (which is used in different ways by Paul) here is used like Jesus did when James and John wanted to have the seats of prominence in His kingdom - that it is a reference to martyrdom. Paul goes on to show that the dead are raised to live with Christ. Thus, he concludes: *1 Cor. 15:[57] But thanks be to God, which giveth us the victory through our Lord Jesus Christ.[58] Therefore, my beloved brethren, be ye steadfast, unmoveable, always abounding in the work of the Lord, forasmuch as ye know that your labour is not in vain in the Lord.*

In 2 Corinthians, we see the cross of the Christian. We are

linked with Christ in His sufferings. He never abandons us while we are suffering. *2 Corinthians 1:[3] Blessed be God, even the Father of our Lord Jesus Christ, the Father of mercies, and the God of all comfort;[4] Who comforteth us in all our tribulation, that we may be able to comfort them which are in any trouble, by the comfort wherewith we ourselves are comforted of God.[5] For as the sufferings of Christ abound in us, so our consolation also aboundeth by Christ.[6] And whether we be afflicted, it is for your consolation and salvation, which is effectual in the enduring of the same sufferings which we also suffer: or whether we be comforted, it is for your consolation and salvation. [7] And our hope of you is stedfast, knowing, that as ye are partakers of the sufferings, so shall ye be also of the consolation.[8] For we would not, brethren, have you ignorant of our trouble which came to us in Asia, that we were pressed out of measure, above strength, insomuch that we despaired even of life:[9] But we had the sentence of death in ourselves, that we should not trust in ourselves, but in God which raiseth the dead:[10] Who delivered us from so great a death, and doth deliver: in whom we trust that he will yet deliver us.*

Paul identified himself with the sufferings of Christ, just as Christ had identified with the sufferings of His people. Christ never leaves us or abandons us in our suffering for Him. But the false apostles preached a different gospel, perhaps similar to the "word of faith" gospel today. Their gospel, which is a gospel without self-sacrifice, without a cross, and without suffering, is truly another gospel and presents another Jesus.

Paul's sufferings are seen differently by the world than by the people of God. *2 Corinthians 2:[14] Now thanks be unto God, which **always** causeth us to triumph in Christ, and maketh manifest the savour of his knowledge by us in every place.[15] For we are unto God a sweet savour of Christ, in them that are saved, and in them that perish:[16] To the one we are the savour of death unto death; and to the other the savour of life unto life. And who is sufficient for these things?[17] For we are not as* *many, which corrupt the word of God: but as of sincerity, but as of God, in the sight of God speak we in Christ.*

The Christian sees the triumph of those behind Christ. The world in general does not. But the Holy Spirit opens the eyes of the unbeliever to the truth of the gospel when His people demonstrate Christlike character. Therefore, if the church is to be truly faithful to its calling, the church can never be truly "seeker-sensitive."

Paul's sufferings are necessary to manifest Christ. *2 Cor. 4:[5] For we preach not ourselves, but Christ Jesus the Lord; and ourselves your servants for Jesus' sake.[6] For God, who commanded the light to shine out of darkness, hath shined in our hearts, to give the light of the knowledge of the glory of God in the face of Jesus Christ.[7] But we have this treasure in earthen vessels, that the excellency of the power may be of God, and not of us.* We need to remember that it is the **gospel** that is glorious, and not the **messenger**. Paul calls the messenger a clay pot. Jesus was not attractive to the world and His messengers will not be attractive either.

2 Cor. 4:[8] We are troubled on every side, yet not distressed; we are perplexed, but not in despair;[9] Persecuted, but not forsaken; cast down, but not destroyed;[10] Always bearing about in the body the dying of the Lord Jesus, that the life also of Jesus might be made manifest in our body.[11] For we which live are always delivered unto death for Jesus' sake, that the life also of Jesus might be made manifest in our mortal flesh.[12] So then death worketh in us, but life in you. Jesus was dying throughout life as He was tempted and rejected. Paul sees himself also dying a bit day by day. This daily dying allows the life of Christ to be manifest in our bodies. *2 Cor. 4:[16] For which cause we faint not; but though our outward man perish, yet the inward man is renewed day by day.[17] For our light affliction, which is but for a moment, worketh for us a far more exceeding and eternal weight of glory;[18] While we look not at the things which are seen, but at the things which are not seen:*

for the things which are seen are temporal; but the things which are not seen are eternal. Paul contrasts his afflictions, which he terms light and temporary, with the eternal weight of glory which awaits him in the future. It will be worth it all.

2 Cor. 5:[1] For we know that if our earthly house of this tabernacle were dissolved, we have a building of God, an house not made with hands, eternal in the heavens.[2] For in this we groan, earnestly desiring to be clothed upon with our house which is from heaven:[3] If so be that being clothed we shall not be found naked.[4] For we that are in this tabernacle do groan, being burdened: not for that we would be unclothed, but clothed upon, that mortality might be swallowed up of life.[5] Now he that hath wrought us for the selfsame thing is God, who also hath given unto us the earnest of the Spirit. [6] Therefore we are always confident, knowing that, whilst we are at home in the body, we are absent from the Lord:[7] (For we walk by faith, not by sight:)[8] We are confident, I say, and willing rather to be absent from the body, and to be present with the Lord[9] Wherefore we labour, that, whether present or absent, we may be accepted of him.[10] For we must all appear before the judgment seat of Christ; that every one may receive the things done in his body, according to that he hath done, whether it be good or bad. Our true home is in heaven. But now we work so that when we arrive, we will be acceptable. Our works do not earn heaven, but they do open the door to rewards there, primarily that reward of ruling with Him.

With this in mind, we remember that it is possible for God and man to be reconciled, and God has given us this message. We are His ambassadors and must preach His message. And we preach it through the same method as Christ — through self-sacrifice and suffering rather than self-exaltation.

Paul's suffering brings a unique perspective to his ministry. He lives what he preaches. His life reinforces the message he brings. Thus, Paul's sufferings prove that he is God's messenger. *2 Corinthians 6:[3] Giving no offense in anything that the ministry be not blamed: [4] But in all things approving ourselves as ministers of God, in much patience, in afflictions, in necessities, in distresses, [5] In stripes, in imprisonments, in tumults, in labors, in watchings, in fastings, [6] By pureness, by knowledge, by long-suffering, by kindness, by the Holy Ghost, by love unfeigned, [7] By the word of truth, by the power of God, by the armor of righteousness on the right hand and on the left, [8] By honor and dishonor, by evil report and good report: as deceivers, and yet true; [9] As unknown, and yet well known, as dying, and behold we live; as chastened, and not killed; [10] As sorrowful, and yet always rejoicing, as poor, yet making many rich; as having nothing, and yet possessing all things. . . .* The message is credible because the messenger is credible. He lives his message.

Once again, Paul gives his credentials as a servant of the living God in chapter eleven. *2 Corinthians 11:[23] Are they ministers of Christ? (I speak as a fool) I am more; in labours more abundant, in stripes above measure, in prisons more frequent, in deaths oft.[24] Of the Jews five times received I forty stripes save one.[25] Thrice was I beaten with rods, once was I stoned, thrice I suffered shipwreck, a night and a day I have been in the deep;[26] In journeyings often, in perils of waters, in perils of robbers, in perils by mine own countrymen, in perils by the heathen, in perils in the city, in perils in the wilderness, in perils in the sea, in perils among false brethren; [27] In weariness and painfulness, in watchings often, in hunger and thirst, in fastings often, in cold and nakedness.[28] Beside those things that are without, that which cometh upon me daily, the care of all the churches.[29] Who is weak, and I am not weak? who is offended, and I burn not?[30] If I must needs glory, I will glory of the things which concern mine infirmities. [31] The God and Father of our Lord Jesus Christ, which is blessed for evermore, knoweth that I lie not.* Notice that Paul boasts not of his successes, but glories in his infirmities.

Richard Wurmbrand had an experience which reinforced his

message as well. When he arrived in the USA to speak about those suffering persecution, one day he passed a large organized leftist group where a Presbyterian minister was addressing the crowd. The minister was praising communism. He jumped on the podium, strode to the microphone, and took over. "You are a Judas," he told the minister. "How can you praise the tormentors when many believers are being tortured for their faith. You know nothing of communism. I am a doctor of communism." The minister replied: "There is no such thing as a doctor of communism." "I will show you my credentials," Wurmbrand said, and stripped off his shirt. He showed the deep scars that were over his torso from the tortures of the communists. He too had his credentials.

By Amy Carmichael:

Have you no scar? No hidden scar on foot, or side, or hand?

I hear you sung as mighty in the land.

I hear them hail your bright ascendant star.

Have you no scar?

Have you no wound?

Yet, I was wounded by the archers, spent, leaned me against the tree to die,

and rent -- by ravenous beasts that encompassed me

I swooned.

Have you no wound?

No wound? No scar?

Yes, as the master shall the servant be,

and pierced are the feet that follow Me,

but yours are whole.

Can he have followed far -- who has no wound? No scar?

Can she have followed far -- who has no wound? No scar?[18]

Again we think of Paul's comment: *Gal. 6:[17] From henceforth let no man trouble me: for I bear in my body the marks of the Lord Jesus.* There were stripes from the five times that the Jews gave him 39 stripes, the most they could do according to the law. There were stripes from the 3 times that the Romans beat him with rods. To that we add the times he was in shackles. Indeed - Paul carried on his body the marks of Christ.

In the trials, Paul discovered that God's grace in his weakness is sufficient. *2 Corinthians 12:[7] And lest I should be exalted above measure through the abundance of the revelations, there was given to me a thorn in the flesh, the messenger of Satan to buffet me, lest I should be exalted above measure.[8] For this thing I besought the Lord thrice, that it might depart from me.[9] And he said unto me, My grace is sufficient for thee: for my strength is made perfect in weakness. Most gladly therefore will I rather glory in my infirmities, that the power of Christ may rest upon me.[10] Therefore I take pleasure in infirmities, in reproaches, in necessities, in persecutions, in distresses for Christ's sake: for when I am weak, then am I strong.* God's grace is actually magnified in my weakness. This is a fundamental truth, and we must never forget it.

In summarizing 1 & 2 Corinthians, Paul shows us that he has endured all to spread the gospel of Jesus Christ. He has this treasure (the gospel) in an earthen vessel. During this time, although his outer man (his physical body) is perishing, his inner man is being renewed. This inner man shall appear before the judgment seat of Christ (2 Cor. 5:8-10).

We need to remember that our "light afflictions" produce in us an eternal weight of glory! We are called to the fellowship of His sufferings, but also we are called to share in His glory. As we are tested through our trials, we are changed to become more capable of ruling with Him. Our reward in heaven will include greater responsibility through our godly response to persecution and trials.

Persecution in Romans

In Romans, we learn that persecution prepares us for the responsibilities that we will inherit so that we will not be put to shame in the future. *Romans 5:[3] And not only so, but we glory in tribulations also: knowing that tribulation to work and patience, [4] And patience, experience, and experience, hope: [5] And hope maketh not ashamed, because the love of God is shed abroad in our hearts by the Holy Ghost which is given unto us. . . .* Our experiences here on earth will prepare us for future life with God in heaven. It is not simply that we will go to heaven, but that we will develop the character proving that we are worthy to be trusted with an inheritance.

The last half of Romans 8 speaks much about life in the Spirit in the framework of persecution. *Romans 8:[16] The Spirit itself beareth witness with our spirit, that we are the children of God:[17] And if children, then heirs; heirs of God, and joint-heirs with Christ; if so be that we suffer with him, that we may be also glorified together.* Thus our inheritance is contingent upon our suffering with him. If we don't share in His sufferings, we don't share in His glory.

Christ Himself was appointed to suffer and then to be glorified. *Luke 24:[26] Ought not Christ to have suffered these things, and to enter into his glory? 1 Peter 1:[10] Of which salvation the prophets have inquired and searched diligently, who prophesied of the grace that should come unto you:[11] Searching what, or what manner of time the Spirit of Christ which was in them did signify, when it testified beforehand the sufferings of Christ, and the glory that should follow.*

This is clearly shown in *Philippians 2:[5] Let this mind be in you, which was also in Christ Jesus:[6] Who, being in the form of God, thought it not robbery to be equal with God:[7] But made himself of no reputation, and took upon him the form of a servant, and was made in the likeness of men:[8] And being found in fashion as a man, he humbled himself, and became obedient unto death, even the death of the cross.[9] Wherefore God also hath highly exalted him, and given him a name which is above every name:[10] That at the name of Jesus every knee should bow, of things in heaven, and things in earth, and things under the earth;[11] And that every tongue should confess that Jesus Christ is Lord, to the glory of God the Father.* His heirs will share in His suffering, and thus demonstrate their worthiness to partner with Him in eternity.

Our rewards are not material goods but being put in positions of authority in heaven. We do not actually earn these positions. They are given by His grace. We are receiving our inheritance. No one earns an inheritance. It is given by the generosity of his father. Likewise, we do not earn our positions in heaven, but we do show our worthiness to have such responsibility. God uses trials to shape us into His image. God wants to develop us into children who are blameless, unselfish, enduring, faithful, self-giving and obedient. We must align our method of ministry with His method of the cross if we are to share in His inheritance, which is also to share in His glory. The sufferings are not to be compared with the glory which we receive from Him. *Romans 8:[18] For I reckon that the sufferings of this present time are not worthy to be compared with the glory which shall be revealed in us.*

We groan for release from suffering along with all of the creation. The fall affected not only Adam and Eve, but creation itself. Furthermore, God has given us the Holy Spirit to help us to pray. *Romans 8:[19] For the earnest expectation of the creature waiteth for the manifestations of the sons of God. [20] For the creature was made subject to vanity, not willingly, but by reason of him who hath subjected the same in hope. [21] Because the creature itself also shall be delivered from the bondage of corruption into the glorious liberty of the children of God. [22] For we know that the whole creation groaneth and travaileth in pain together until now. [23] And not only they, but ourselves also which have the first fruits of the Spirit, even we ourselves groan within ourselves, waiting for the adoption, to wit; the redemption of our bodies... [26] Likewise the Spirit also helpeth our infirmities: for we know not what we should pray for as we ought: but the Spirit itself maketh intercession for us with groanings which cannot be uttered. [27] And he that searches the hearts knows what is in the mind of the Spirit, because he maketh intercession for the saints according to the will of God.* But God gives all of this suffering for our own good. God's plan is never hindered by persecution. He uses persecution to make us like Himself, and the results are certain.

Romans 8:[28] And we know that all things work together for good to them that love God, to them who are called according to his purpose. [29] For whom he did foreknow, he also did predestinate to be conformed to the image of his son, that he might be the firstborn among many brethren. [30] Moreover whom he predestinated, them he also called: and whom he called, them he also justified: and whom he justified, them he also glorified. God's plan is certain, and our triumph is sure. God is conforming us to be like Jesus. And we see that this is so secure that the glorification is written as if it has already occurred. We need not fear. We need not despair.

In Romans 8:31-39, we are in context of those who were suffering from persecution for Christ's sake. Nothing can separate us from the love of God, including persecution. *Romans 8:[31] What shall we then say to these things? If God be for us, who can be against us? [32] He that spared not his own Son, but delivered him up for us all, how shall he not with him also freely give us all things? [33] Who shall lay anything to the charge of God's elect? It is God that justifeth. [34] Who is he that condemneth? It is Christ that died, yea, rather, that is risen again, who is even at the right hand of God, who also maketh intercession for us. [35] Who shall separate us from the love of Christ? Shall tribulation, or distress, or persecution, or famine, or nakedness, or peril, or sword? [36] As it is written, For thy sake we are killed all the day long; we are accounted as sheep for the slaughter. [37] Nay, in all the things we are more than conquerors through him that loved us. [38] For I am persuaded that neither death, nor life, nor angels, nor principalities, nor powers, or things present, nor things to come, [39] Nor height nor depth, nor any other creature, shall be able to separate us from the love of God, which is in Christ Jesus our Lord.* In the face of persecution, we are still more than conquerors.

How should we react to persecution? *Romans 12:[14] Bless them which persecute you: bless, and curse not.[15] Rejoice with them that do rejoice, and weep with them that weep.[16] Be of the same mind one toward another. Mind not high things, but condescend to men of low estate. Be not wise in your own conceits.[17] Recompense to no man evil for evil. Provide things honest in the sight of all men.[18] If it be possible, as much as lieth in you, live peaceably with all men.[19] Dearly beloved, avenge not yourselves, but rather give place unto wrath: for it is written, Vengeance is mine; I will repay, saith the Lord.[20] Therefore if thine enemy hunger, feed him; if he thirst, give him drink: for in so doing thou shalt heap coals of fire on his head.[21] Be not overcome of evil, but overcome evil with good.*

It is quite clear that we should not react in the flesh, returning evil for evil. Instead, we should win over evil with good. This we cannot do in our own strength, but this is a manifestation of the power of God in our lives when we are controlled by the Holy Spirit. This attitude is powerful. Then the light of the gospel shines in the darkness of the world.

Persecution in Galatians and the Prison Epistles

In the book of Galatians also, we find that persecution occurs as we serve the Lord Jesus Christ. *Galatians 6:[12] As many as desired to make a fair show in the flesh, they constrain you to be circumcised: only lest they should suffer persecution for the cross is Christ. . . . [14] But God forbid that I should glory, save in the cross of Jesus Christ, by whom the world is crucified to me, and I unto the world.* It is the cross that separates

81

me from the system of the world. The cross is also an offense to the world, and they will reject me. And as we noted above, Paul bears the marks of Christ on his body. *Galatians 6:[17] From henceforth let no man trouble me: for I bear in my body the marks of the Lord Jesus.* As noted above, I picture Paul exposing his back, scarred from five Jewish lashings and three Roman whippings. The marks of his torture were the marks of Jesus Christ.

In the book of Ephesians, Jesus Christ is a prisoner of Christ, and not of Rome. First, he prays that the believers will know their inheritance in glory. *Ephesians 1:[15] Wherefore I also, after I heard of your faith in the Lord Jesus, and love unto all the saints,[16] Cease not to give thanks for you, making mention of you in my prayers;[17] That the God of our Lord Jesus Christ, the Father of glory, may give unto you the spirit of wisdom and revelation in the knowledge of him:[18] The eyes of your understanding being enlightened; that ye may know what is the hope of his calling, and what the riches of the glory of his inheritance in the saints,[19] And what is the exceeding greatness of his power to usward who believe, according to the working of his mighty power,[20] Which he wrought in Christ, when he raised him from the dead, and set him at his own right hand in the heavenly places,[21] Far above all principality, and power, and might, and dominion, and every name that is named, not only in this world, but also in that which is to come:[22] And hath put all things under his feet, and gave him to be the head over all things to the church,[23] Which is his body, the fulness of him that filleth all in all.* In Christ, we are in a position of victory against Satan and his evil spirits. We must also consider our wonderful inheritance in Christ. This is a tremendous encouragement in times of persecution. God is molding us to be fit for that inheritance which He wrought in Christ.

God revealed to Paul the mystery of unity between Jew and Gentiles. He is in prison suffering for that message. *Ephesians 3:[1] For this I Paul, the prisoner of Jesus Christ for you*

Gentiles,[2] If ye have heard of the dispensation of the grace of God which is given me to you-ward:[3] How that by revelation he made known unto me the mystery; (as I wrote afore in few words,[4] Whereby, when ye read, ye may understand my knowledge in the mystery of Christ)[5] Which in other ages was not made known unto the sons of men, as it is now revealed unto his holy apostles and prophets by the Spirit;[6] That the Gentiles should be fellow heirs, and of the same body, and partakers of his promise in Christ by the gospel: [7] Whereof I was made a minister, according to the gift of the grace of God given unto me by the effectual working of his power.[8] Unto me, who am less than the least of all saints, is this grace given, that I should preach among the Gentiles the unsearchable riches of Christ;[9] And to make all men see what is the fellowship of the mystery, which from the beginning of the world hath been hid in God, who created all things by Jesus Christ:[10] To the intent that now unto the principalities and powers in heavenly places might be known by the church the manifold wisdom of God. God revealed to Paul that the Gentiles (you and I) have an inheritance in the unsearchable riches in Christ. All the powers of heaven and hell shall see this come to pass.

Paul was suffering for the message he delivered. This suffering is the Ephesians' glory. He prayed that nothing would uproot their love for Christ. *Ephesians 3:[13] Wherefore I desire that ye faint not at my tribulations for you, which is your glory.[14] For this cause I bow my knees unto the Father of our Lord Jesus Christ,[15] Of whom the whole family in heaven and earth is named,[16] That he would grant you, according to the riches of his glory, to be strengthened with might by his Spirit in the inner man;[17] That Christ may dwell in your hearts by faith; that ye, being rooted and grounded in love,[18] May be able to comprehend with all saints what is the breadth, and length, and depth, and height;[19] And to know the love of Christ, which passeth knowledge, that ye might be filled with all the fullness of God.[20] Now unto him that is able to do exceeding abundantly above all that we ask or think, according to the power that worketh in us,[21] Unto him be glory in the church by Christ Jesus throughout all ages, world without end. Amen.* This, of course, will bring great glory to God as well. Paul had warned the elders from the church of Ephesus of coming persecution when he parted from them on the beach in Acts 20. Now he prays for them to be stable.

Thus, we must walk worthy of our calling. This worthiness will be shown as unity among believers. *Ephesians 4:[1] I therefore, the prisoner of the Lord, beseech you that ye walk worthy of the vocation wherewith ye are called,[2] With all lowliness and meekness, with longsuffering, forbearing one another in love;[3] Endeavouring to keep the unity of the Spirit in the bond of peace.[4] There is one body, and one Spirit, even as ye are called in one hope of your calling;[5] One Lord, one faith, one baptism,[6] One God and Father of all, who is above all, and through all, and in you all.* Notice that the characteristics of walking worthy are meekness, longsuffering, and forbearance in love.

In Ephesians 6:10-20, he says that we must be strong in the Lord despite trials and suffering. The real battle is against Satan. *Ephesians 6:[10] And finally, my brethren, be strong in the Lord, and in the power of his might. [11] Put on the whole armor of God, that you might be able to stand against the wiles of the devil. [12] For we wrestle not against flesh and blood, but against principalities, against powers, against the rulers of darkness of this world, against spiritual wickedness in high places. [13] Wherefore take unto you the whole armor of God, that ye may be able to withstand in the evil day, and having done all, to stand.* We need to take all the armor of God to be able to withstand the onslaughts of the enemy. But God will make us victorious.

Ephesians 6:[14] Stand therefore, having your loins girt about with truth, and having on the breastplate of righteousness; [15] And your feet shod with the preparation of the gospel of peace; [16] Above all, taking the shield of faith, wherewith ye shall be able to quench all the fiery darts of the wicked. When we face hostility, we must arm ourselves with the truth. We must do right and trust in the resources of the Lord.

Ephesians 6:[17] And take the helmet of salvation, and the sword of the Spirit, which is the word of God: The Lord Himself provides salvation and the word of God, which we take and use. But we must depend totally on the Lord and prayer. *6:[18] Praying always with all prayer and supplication in the Spirit, and watching thereunto with all perseverance and supplication for all saints; [19] And for me, that utterance may be given unto me, that I may open my mouth boldly, to make known the mystery of the gospel. [20] For which I am an ambassador in bonds: therefore I may speak boldly, as I ought to speak.* God has given us enough resources to stand, but we must take them and stand. Paul is an ambassador in chains, and he must deliver the message of the King of Kings.

The book of Philippians is also one of the prison epistles. In Philippians chapter 1, we see that we have received the gift (grace) of being able to suffer for Christ. This grace transforms us as sufferers to be sacrificial givers of the gospel to others. *Philippians 1:[5] For your fellowship in the gospel from the first day until now;[6] Being confident of this very thing, that he which hath begun a good work in you will perform it until the day of Jesus Christ:[7] Even as it is meet for me to think this of you all, because I have you in my heart; inasmuch as both in my bonds, and in the defense and confirmation of the gospel, ye all are partakers of my grace.* We receive this grace as participants in spreading the gospel. And Paul is confident that God is busy transforming our lives and will continue to transform them to make us like Jesus.

The imprisonment of Paul accomplished three things. The non-Christians knew why he was imprisoned. The Christians took heart as he saw how he responded to the imprisonment. And the gospel was preached throughout even to Caesar's household. *Philippians 1:[12] But I would ye should understand, brethren, that the things which happened unto me have fallen out rather unto the furtherance of the gospel;[13] So that my bonds in Christ are manifest in all the palace, and in all other places;[14] And many of the brethren in the Lord, waxing confident by my bonds, are much more bold to speak the word without fear.[15] Some indeed preach Christ even of envy and strife; and some also of good will:[16] The one preach Christ of contention, not sincerely, supposing to add affliction to my bonds:[17] But the other of love, knowing that I am set for the defence of the gospel.[18] What then? notwithstanding, every way, whether in pretence, or in truth, Christ is preached; and I therein do rejoice, yea, and will rejoice.*

Paul rejoices in his imprisonment. *Phil. 1:[20] According to my earnest expectation and my hope, that in nothing I shall be ashamed, but that with all boldness, as always, so now also Christ shall be magnified in my body, whether it be by life, or by death.[21] For to me to live is Christ, and to die is gain.[22] But if I live in the flesh, this is the fruit of my labour: yet what I shall choose I wot not.[23] For I am in a strait betwixt two, having a desire to depart, and to be with Christ; which is far better:[24] Nevertheless to abide in the flesh is more needful for you.* Paul's priorities were demonstrated as he accepted whatever the Lord found best. He shows that joy is not dependent on one's circumstances, but it is dependent on one's priorities!

Paul prays for the Philippian believers to allow suffering and persecution to mold them into the image of Christ. He looks at persecution as a gift of God. *Philippians 1:[27] Only let your conversation be as it becometh the gospel of Christ: that whether I come and see you, or else be absent, I may hear of your affairs, that ye stand fast in one spirit, with one mind striving together for the faith of the gospel;[28] And in nothing terrified by your adversaries: which is to them an evident token of perdition, but to you of salvation, and that of God.[29] For unto you it is* **given** *in the behalf of Christ, not only to believe on him, but also to suffer for his sake.*

God is busy molding us into the image of Christ so that we will be worthy of our inheritance. Here he attacks self-centered living. *Philippians 2:[1] If there be therefore any consolation in Christ, if any comfort of love, if any fellowship of the Spirit, if any bowels and mercies,[2] Fulfil ye my joy, that ye be likeminded, having the same love, being of one accord, of one mind.[3] Let nothing be done through strife or vainglory; but in lowliness of mind let each esteem other better than them- selves.[4] Look not every man on his own things, but every man also on the things of others.* If we are to be trusted by God, we must be concerned first of all for God Himself, and then also for others.

God has given us the mind of Christ, and we must think like Him. *Philippians 2:[5] Let this mind be in you, which was also in Christ Jesus:[6] Who, being in the form of God, thought it not robbery to be equal with God:[7] But made himself of no reputation, and took upon him the form of a servant, and was made in the likeness of men:[8] And being found in fashion as a man, he humbled himself, and became obedient unto death, even the death of the cross.[9] Wherefore God also hath highly exalted him, and given him a name which is above every name:[10] That at the name of Jesus every knee should bow, of things in heaven, and things in earth, and things under the earth;[11] And that every tongue should confess that Jesus Christ is Lord, to the glory of God the Father.*

God is a God of love. It is part of His nature to be self-sacrificing. He is not a God who wishes to get more for Himself, but empties Himself to meet the needs of others. So, the life and death of Christ is perfectly compatible with His nature as God. And as such, He is indeed worthy of all worship, power and authority. His suffering is linked with His glory.

We must work out the implications of this in our lives. The power comes from Him. We are not earning rewards but developing a character that is worthy of His life in us. *Philippians 2:[12] Wherefore, my beloved, as ye have always*

87

obeyed, not as in my presence only, but now much more in my absence, work out your own salvation with fear and trembling.[13] For it is God which worketh in you both to will and to do of his good pleasure.[14] Do all things without murmurings and disputings:[15] That ye may be blameless and harmless, the sons of God, without rebuke, in the midst of a crooked and perverse nation, among whom ye shine as lights in the world;[16] Holding forth the word of life; that I may rejoice in the day of Christ, that I have not run in vain, neither laboured in vain. Paul has poured his life into them, and wants to see them receive a full reward, which is also a proof of his ministry.

In chapter 3, Paul begins by showing how he had valued his religious heritage at first, but compared to being in Christ, he found it to be rubbish. *Philippians 3:[5] Circumcised the eighth day, of the stock of Israel, of the tribe of Benjamin, an Hebrew of the Hebrews; as touching the law, a Pharisee; [6] Concerning zeal, persecuting the church; touching the righteousness which is in the law, blameless. [7] But what things were gain to me, those I counted loss for Christ.[8] Yea doubtless, and I count all things but loss for the excellency of the knowledge of Christ Jesus my Lord: for whom I have suffered the loss of all things, and do count them but dung, that I may win Christ,[9] And be found in him, not having mine own righteousness, which is of the law, but that which is through the faith of Christ, the righteousness which is of God by faith:[10] That I may know him, and the power of his resurrection, and the fellowship of his sufferings, being made conformable unto his death;[11] If by any means I might attain unto the resurrection of the dead.* Paul makes it clear that righteousness is not found through religious law, but through a personal relationship with Christ. That relationship occurs through faith, and not by works.

In Philippians 3:10, Paul desires to know Christ personally. How must he do that? *3:[10] that I might know him, and the power of his resurrection, and the fellowship of his sufferings, being made conformable unto his death;[11] If by any means I might attain unto the resurrection of the dead.* When he uses the term stating that he might attain the resurrection of the dead, it is a special word, and might possibly refer to a special type of reward. He is striving for it, has not yet obtained it, but seeks it. *Philippians 3:[12] Not as though I had already attained, either were already perfect: but I follow after, if that I may apprehend that for which also I am apprehended of Christ Jesus.[13] Brethren, I count not myself to have apprehended: but this one thing I do, forgetting those things which are behind, and reaching forth unto those things which are before,[14] I press toward the mark for the prize of the high calling of God in Christ Jesus.*

In contrast to this, there are those who are the enemies of the cross and set their minds on earthly things. *Philippians 3:[17] Brethren, be followers together of me, and mark them which walk so as ye have us for an example. [18] (For many walk, of whom I've told you often, and now tell you even weeping, that they are the enemies of the cross of Christ: [19] Whose end is destruction, whose God is their belly, and whose glory is their shame, who mind earthly things.) [20] For our conversation is in heaven; from whence we also look for the Savior, the Lord Jesus Christ: [21] Who shall change our vile body, that it may be fashioned like unto his glorious body, according to the working whereby he is able even to subdue all things unto himself.* Philippi was a Roman colony, and its citizens were proud to be Roman citizens. But Paul shows that our real citizenship as believers is in heaven. He is developing our character, and after our physical death, He will transform our physical bodies so that they are appropriate for life also in heaven and not just on earth.

In Colossians, also written in prison, Paul shows us that his work is Christ's work. Christ works through those who make His goals their goals. This demands labor and agony. The gospel cannot be preached, and the people of God cannot be gathered into congregations within the nations, unless there are individuals here and there completing what is lacking in Christ's afflictions so that the task might be accomplished. *Colossians 1:[24] Who now rejoice in my sufferings for you, and fill up that which is behind of the afflictions of Christ in my flesh for his body's sake, which is the church:[25] Whereof I am made a minister, according to the dispensation of God which is given to me for you, to fulfill the word of God;[26] Even the mystery which hath been hid from ages and from generations, but now is made manifest to his saints:[27] To whom God would make known what is the riches of the glory of this mystery among the Gentiles; which is Christ in you, the hope of glory:[28] Whom we preach, warning every man, and teaching every man in all wisdom; that we may present every man perfect in Christ Jesus:[29] Whereunto I also labour, striving according to his working, which worketh in me mightily.*

These afflictions confront all who deliberately involve themselves in active service for Christ. This is particularly true when they bear public witness to the gospel. Each generation must be willing to endure suffering. Paul's goal is that each man would be presented mature in Christ. Christ works in and through him to make that goal possible.

Persecution in the Pastoral Epistles

Timothy is Paul's right-hand man, who will basically take over after his death. He is encouraged in *1 Tim. 6:[12] Fight the good fight of faith, lay hold on eternal life, whereunto thou art also called, and hast professed a good profession before many witnesses.[13] I give thee charge in the sight of God, who quickeneth all things, and before Christ Jesus, who before Pontius Pilate witnessed a good confession;[14] That thou keep this commandment without spot, unrebukeable, until the appearing of our Lord Jesus Christ.* We are not certain when Timothy was a confessor (the term used for a witness being tried, especially for his faith). However, Paul encourages him to keep on keeping on. When facing persecution, it is a temptation to quit the battle, or change your message or lifestyle to accommodate those around you. Timothy is to persist in the battle.

2 Timothy is Paul's last letter written while in prison facing death. It is written to encourage his key disciple, Timothy. He gives him great encouragement to persevere despite persecution. God gives greater grace to be victorious over the sufferings which we must endure. We must offer love to those who do not deserve it. This occurs mostly with self-sacrifice. We must seek the best for those who seek to harm us. The greatest example of all is Jesus Christ.

Thus, God gives us a spirit of self-control in place of a spirit of fear. *2 Timothy 1:[7] For God hath not given us the spirit of fear; but of power, and of love, and of a sound mind.[8] Be not thou therefore ashamed of the testimony of our Lord, nor of me his prisoner: but be thou partaker of the afflictions of the gospel according to the power of God;[9] Who hath saved us, and called us with an holy calling, not according to our works, but according to his own purpose and grace, which was given us in Christ Jesus before the world began.* Timothy must not be afraid of the trials, or be ashamed of Paul, but to speak out boldly as a Christian. God will give us the power we need to witness. He will give us the love that casts out fear. And He will give us the wisdom and self-control that we need. Paul warns Timothy not to be ashamed of his suffering but to join in it.

2 Timothy 1:[12] For the which cause I also suffer these things: nevertheless I am not ashamed: for I know whom I have believed, and am persuaded that he is able to keep that which I have committed unto him against that day.[13] Hold fast the form of sound words, which thou hast heard of me, in faith and love which is in Christ Jesus.[14] That good thing which was committed unto thee keep by the Holy Ghost which dwelleth in us. The persecuted church is not a church of victims! If they are faithful to Scripture, they go forth in the power of God, believing that suffering is not the worst thing that can happen to them. Thus, we must be faithful. The reward comes at the end. If we die with Him, we will live with Him. We must be faithful, but even when we fail, we must come back to God, because He will never fail us.

Timothy must persevere despite sufferings, for the rewards will follow. *2 Tim. 2:[3] Thou therefore endure hardness, as a good soldier of Jesus Christ.[4] No man that warreth entangleth himself with the affairs of this life; that he may please him who hath chosen him to be a soldier.[5] And if a man also strive for masteries, yet is he not crowned, except he strive lawfully.[6] The husbandman that laboureth must be first partaker of the fruits.[7] Consider what I say; and the Lord give thee understanding in all things.* The soldier, the athlete, and the farmer must all discipline themselves to work in the proper way so that they may receive rewards for what they have done.

We must continue to serve the Lord. *2 Tim. 2:[8] Remember that Jesus Christ of the seed of David was raised from the dead according to my gospel:[9] Wherein I suffer trouble, as an evil doer, even unto bonds; but the word of God is not bound.[10] Therefore I endure all things for the elect's sakes, that they may also obtain the salvation which is in Christ Jesus with eternal glory.[11] It is a faithful saying: For if we be dead with him, we shall also live with him:[12] If we suffer, we shall also reign with him: if we deny him, he also will deny us:[13] If we believe not, yet he abideth faithful: he cannot deny himself.* Paul is persecuted because he preaches the gospel and the resurrection of the Lord Jesus Christ. Although he is in prison, bound by chains and facing death, the word is not bound. And if we die with Him, we will live with Him. If we suffer with Him, we will reign with Him, but if we deny Him, then He will deny us. We will be disapproved.

2 Timothy 3:[10] But thou hast fully known my doctrine, manner of life, purpose, faith, longsuffering, charity, patience,[11] Persecutions, afflictions, which came unto me at Antioch, at Iconium, at Lystra; what persecutions I endured: but out of them all the Lord delivered me.[12] Yea, and all that will live godly in Christ Jesus shall suffer persecution.[13] But evil men and seducers shall wax worse and worse, deceiving, and being deceived. Timothy knew the life that Paul had lived.

Timothy was fully aware of the persecution Paul had suffered, including the stoning at his own home town, Lystra.

But it is not just Paul who will suffer. All the godly will be persecuted, but false teachers will get worse and worse to avoid persecution. These false teachers re-fashion their message and their life to avoid paying the cost of following Jesus Christ. Paul suffers to carry the gospel to the lost. Suffering in itself has no great value but suffering for Christ will bring great rewards.

Paul said that he was the drink-offering given in thankful-ness for the forgiveness of sins. This offering is the last part of worship after the burnt offering and meal offering. Paul points out that this work was done by the Lord and it is His work and He deserves praise. However, Paul gets the crown of righteous-ness, not by his own work and but by his total dependence on the work of Jesus Christ. *2 Tim. 4:[6] For I am now ready to be offered, and the time of my departure is at hand.[7] I have fought a good fight, I have finished my course, I have kept the faith:[8] Henceforth there is laid up for me a crown of righteousness, which the Lord, the righteous judge, shall give me at that day: and not to me only, but unto all them also that love his appearing.*

Persecution in Hebrews

In the book of Hebrews, God shows that He has a destiny for man. *Heb. 2:[4] God also bearing them witness, both with signs and wonders, and with divers miracles, and gifts of the Holy Ghost, according to his own will?[5] For unto the angels hath he not put in subjection the world to come, whereof we speak.[6] But one in a certain place testified, saying, What is man, that thou art mindful of him? or the son of man, that thou visitest him?[7] Thou madest him a little lower than the angels; thou crownedst him with glory and honour, and didst set him over the works of thy hands:[8] Thou hast put all things in subjection under his feet. For in that he put all in subjection under him, he left nothing that is not put under him. But now we see not yet all things put under him.*

Thus, God's plan is that man rule the universe with Him. But when man fell, our relationship with God was broken and that rule was no longer feasible. Man did not show that he was worthy to rule with God. But Jesus Christ made it possible for man to have a restored relationship with God. Through Jesus Christ it is possible for man to rule with God forever.

Heb. 2:[9] But we see Jesus, who was made a little lower than the angels for the suffering of death, crowned with glory and honour; that he by the grace of God should taste death for every man.[10] For it became him, for whom are all things, and by whom are all things, in bringing many sons unto glory, to make the captain of their salvation perfect through sufferings.[11] For both he that sanctifieth and they who are sanctified are all of one: for which cause he is not ashamed to call them brethren,[12] Saying, I will declare thy name unto my brethren, in the midst of the church will I sing praise unto thee.

Only through Jesus Christ is it possible to be worthy of His kingdom. Jesus Christ is the captain of our salvation. God has placed us in Christ. Jesus was made mature or perfect through sufferings and we can expect suffering to meet us too. Persecution, suffering, and martyrdom show that we are in Christ's school. Christ will use persecution and suffering for us to gain His image of holiness and righteousness. It is a testing ground to mature faith. Thus, we need to identify with Christ's suffering.

Hebrews 2:[14] Forasmuch then as the children are partakers of flesh and blood, he also himself likewise took part of the same; that through death he might destroy him that had the power of death, that is, the devil;[15] And deliver them who through fear of death were all their lifetime subject to bondage.[16] For verily he took not on him the nature of angels; but he took on him the seed of Abraham.[17] Wherefore in all things it behooved him to be made like unto his brethren, that he might be a merciful and faithful high priest in things pertaining to God, to make reconciliation for the sins of the people.[18] For in that he himself hath suffered being tempted, he is able to succour them that are tempted.

It was necessary for Jesus to take the fashion of a man to free us from the penalty of sin. The wages of sin is death, and if He took the form of an angel, He could not die like a man. He had to have a body with blood that could be shed for us. But He did more than that. He was made like us in all ways. He even underwent suffering and temptation, but never sinned. Thus, He is able to succor us in all our temptations and trials.

God designed man to have authority, but authority under God. Jesus willingly submitted to God in all things. *Hebrews 5:[7] Who in the days of his flesh, when he had offered up prayers and supplications with strong crying and tears unto him that was able to save him from death, and was heard in that he feared;[8] Though he were a Son, yet learned he obedience by the things which he suffered;.* We too are to learn obedience in the things that we suffer. God uses suffering to mold us into the image of Jesus Christ.

We receive many illustrations of suffering for Christ in Hebrews 11. A classic example is that of Moses. *Hebrews 11:[24] By faith Moses, when he was come to years, refused to be called the son of Pharaoh's daughter;[25] Choosing rather to suffer affliction with the people of God, than to enjoy the pleasures of sin for a season;[26] Esteeming the reproach of Christ greater riches than the treasures in Egypt: for he had respect unto the recompence of the reward.* Moses chose suffering rather than incredible riches here on earth as the grandson of Pharoah. *[27] By faith he forsook Egypt, not fearing the wrath of the king: for he endured, as seeing him who is invisible.* Why? He was looking forward to a reward in the future, not here on earth, but in heaven.

The same thing is true of Abraham and Sarah: *Heb. 11:[8] By faith Abraham, when he was called to go out into a place which he should after receive for an inheritance, obeyed; and he went out, not knowing whither he went.[9] By faith he sojourned in the land of promise, as in a strange country, dwelling in tabernacles with Isaac and Jacob, the heirs with him of the same promise:[10] For he looked for a city which hath foundations, whose builder and maker is God.[11] Through faith also Sarah herself received strength to conceive seed, and was delivered of a child when she was past age, because she judged him faithful who had promised.[12] Therefore sprang there even of one, and him as good as dead, so many as the stars of the sky in multitude, and as the sand which is by the sea shore innumerable.[13] These all died in faith, not having received the promises, but having seen them afar off, and were persuaded of them, and embraced them, and confessed that they were strangers and pilgrims on the earth.[14] For they that say such things declare plainly that they seek a country.[15] And truly, if they had been mindful of that country from whence they came out, they might have had opportunity to have returned.[16] But now they desire a better country, that is, an heavenly: wherefore God is not ashamed to be called their God: for he hath prepared for them a city.*

The heroes of Hebrews 11 endure trials and temptations looking for a heavenly reward. Notice the common thread of these heroes. It is the trials and temptations which they endured. *Hebrews 11:[32] And what shall I more say? for the time would fail me to tell of Gideon, and of Barak, and of Samson, and of Jephthae; of David also, and Samuel, and of the prophets:[33] Who through faith subdued kingdoms, wrought righteousness, obtained promises, stopped the mouths of lions,[34] Quenched the violence of fire, escaped the edge of the sword, out of weakness were made strong, waxed valiant in fight, turned to flight the armies of the aliens. [35] Women received their dead raised to life again: and others were tortured, not accepting deliverance; that they might obtain a better resurrection: [36] And others had trial of cruel mockings and scourgings, yea, moreover of bonds and imprisonment:[37] They were stoned, they were sawn asunder, were tempted, were slain with the sword: they wandered about in sheepskins and goatskins; being destitute, afflicted, tormented;38] (Of whom the world was not worthy:) they wandered in deserts, and in mountains, and in dens and caves of the earth. [39] And these all, having obtained a good report through faith, received not the promise: [40] God having provided some better thing for us, that they without us should not be made perfect.*

God uses suffering to develop the character we need. *Hebrews 12:[1] Wherefore seeing we also are compassed about with so great a cloud of witnesses, let us lay aside every weight, and the sin which doth so easily beset us, and let us run with patience the race that is set before us,[2] Looking unto Jesus the author and finisher of our faith; who for the joy that was set before him endured the cross, despising the shame, and is set down at the right hand of the throne of God.[3] For consider him that endured such contradiction of sinners against himself, lest ye be wearied and faint in your minds.[4] Ye have not yet resisted unto blood, striving against sin.* Jesus, who lives in us, showed in His life the victory over suffering and sin. We must look to Him first.

Hebrews 12:[5] And ye have forgotten the exhortation which speaketh unto you as unto children, My son, despise not thou the chastening of the Lord, nor faint when thou art rebuked of him:[6] For whom the Lord loveth he chasteneth, and scourgeth every son whom he receiveth.[7] If ye endure chastening, God dealeth with you as with sons; for what son is he whom the father chasteneth not?[8] But if ye be without chastisement, whereof all are partakers, then are ye bastards, and not sons.[9] Furthermore we have had fathers of our flesh which corrected us, and we gave them reverence: shall we not much rather be in subjection unto the Father of spirits, and live?[10] For they verily for a few days chastened us after their own pleasure; but he for our profit, that we might be partakers of his holiness.[11] Now no chastening for the present seemeth to be joyous, but grievous: nevertheless afterward it yieldeth the peaceable fruit of righteousness unto them which are exercised thereby.[12] Wherefore lift up the hands which hang down, and the feeble knees;[13] And make straight paths for your feet, lest that which is lame be turned out of the way; but let it rather be healed.

We must look unto Jesus. We are reminded that even our human fathers disciplined us for our own good. And God the Father works through suffering and trials to discipline us and to build the right character into us. These trials are not punishment for sins, but the way God works His character into us. Sufferings and trials are proofs that we are God's children enrolled in His school. He perfected Jesus through sufferings, and He is now working the same way in us.

In Hebrews 13, we are reminded that we are all part of the body of Christ. When one part suffers, the whole body suffers. *Hebrews 13:[3] Remember them that are in bonds, as bound with them, and them which suffer adversity, as being yourselves also in the body.* Furthermore, Jesus bore reproach outside the city as did the sin offering outside the camp. We must go to Him. *Hebrews 13:[11] For the bodies of those beasts, whose blood is brought into the sanctuary by the high priest for sin, are burned without the camp.[12] Wherefore Jesus also, that he might sanctify the people with his own blood, suffered without the gate.[13] Let us go forth therefore unto him without the camp, bearing his reproach.*

God will give us the power to do so. *Heb. 13:[20] Now the God of peace, that brought again from the dead our Lord Jesus, that great shepherd of the sheep, through the blood of the everlasting covenant,[21] Make you perfect in every good work to do his will, working in you that which is well-pleasing in his sight, through Jesus Christ; to whom be glory for ever and ever. Amen.*

Persecution in James

In the book of James, we find that God uses trials to produce steadfastness and spiritual maturity. We should therefore consider it all joy. James talks here about all sorts of trials. A righteous man should pray for the wisdom to see things from God's perspective. *James 1:[2] My brethren, count it all joy when ye fall into divers temptations[3] Knowing this, that the trying of your faith worketh patience.[4] But let patience have her perfect work, that ye may be perfect and entire, wanting nothing.[5] If any of you lack wisdom, let him ask of God, that giveth to all men liberally, and upbraideth not; and it shall be given him.[6] But let him ask in faith, nothing wavering. For he that wavereth is like a wave of the sea driven with the wind and tossed.[7] For let not that man think that he shall receive any thing of the Lord.[8] A double minded man is unstable in all his ways.* God does not demean the person who asks for wisdom. But we must ask, trusting Him to give us the wisdom we request.

Thus, we should trust the Lord because He is reliable. We don't fall because of outward trials, but because of inward temptations. These temptations will occur continually. God tests us and permits trials in our lives to strengthen us. But God never tempts us to sin. That comes from our own lusts. *James 1:[12] Blessed is the man that endureth temptation: for when he is tried, he shall receive the crown of life, which the Lord hath promised to them that love him.[13] Let no man say when he is tempted, I am tempted of God: for God cannot be tempted with evil, neither tempteth he any man:[14] But every man is tempted, when he is drawn away of his own lust, and enticed.[15] Then when lust hath conceived, it bringeth forth sin: and sin, when it is finished, bringeth forth death.[16] Do not err, my beloved brethren.[17] Every good gift and every perfect gift is from above, and cometh down from the Father of lights, with whom is no variableness, neither shadow of turning.[18] Of his own will begat he us with the word of truth, that we should be a kind of firstfruits of his creatures.* God is good to all who call on him. He gives with an open hand and, ultimately, all good gifts are from Him.

Persecution in First and Second Peter

1 Peter was probably written just before the persecution which began with Nero. He warns the believers that they must be prepared for trials and testing. But the persecution, although it comes from Satan, is permitted by the grace of God. As we suffer wrongfully for Christ's sake, then we walk in His steps. As we follow Christ day by day, we develop obedience and the character necessary to withstand the tests which God permits in our lives. *1 Peter 2:[19] For this is thankworthy, if a man for conscience toward God endure grief, suffering wrongfully.[20] For what glory is it, if, when ye be buffeted for your faults, ye shall take it patiently? but if, when ye do well, and suffer for it, ye take it patiently, this is acceptable with God.[21] For even hereunto were ye called: because Christ also suffered for us, leaving us an example, that ye should follow his steps:[22] Who did no sin, neither was guile found in his mouth:[23] Who, when he was reviled, reviled not again; when he suffered, he threatened not; but committed himself to him that judgeth righteously.*

In chapter 3, Peter continues to encourage the believer to do right even in the face of abuse or persecution. *1 Peter 3:[8] Finally, be ye all of one mind, having compassion one of another, love as brethren, be pitiful, be courteous:[9] Not rendering evil for evil, or railing for railing: but contrariwise blessing; knowing that ye are thereunto called, that ye should inherit a blessing.[10] For he that will love life, and see good days, let him refrain his tongue from evil, and his lips that they speak no guile:[11] Let him eschew evil, and do good; let him seek peace, and ensue it.[12] For the eyes of the Lord are over the righteous, and his ears are open unto their prayers: but the face of the Lord is against them that do evil.[13] And who is he that will harm you, if ye be followers of that which is good?[14] But and if ye suffer for righteousness' sake, happy are ye: and be not afraid of their terror, neither be troubled;[15] But sanctify the Lord God in your hearts: and be ready always to give an answer to every man that asketh you a reason of the hope that is in you with meekness and fear:[16] Having a good conscience; that, whereas they speak evil of you, as of evildoers, they may be ashamed that falsely accuse your good conversation in Christ.[17] For it is better, if the will of God be so, that ye suffer for well doing, than for evil doing.* Our testimony even in the face of provocation can be the very means to bring someone to the Lord. We can expect, however, that a godly lifestyle will precipitate a negative reaction from the world.

In chapter 4, Peter shows us that Christians were rejected because of their lifestyle. Their lifestyle was pure and austere and devoid of idol worship. *1 Peter 4:[1] Forasmuch then as Christ hath suffered for us in the flesh, arm yourselves likewise with the same mind: for he that hath suffered in the flesh hath ceased from sin;[2] That he no longer should live the rest of his time in the flesh to the lusts of men, but to the will of God.[3] For the time past of our life may suffice us to have wrought the will of the Gentiles, when we walked in lasciviousness, lusts, excess of wine, revellings, banquetings, and abominable idolatries:[4] Wherein they think it strange that ye run not with them to the same excess of riot, speaking evil of you:[5] Who shall give account to him that is ready to judge the quick and the dead.[6] For this cause was the gospel preached also to them that are dead, that they might be judged according to men in the flesh, but live according to God in the spirit.*

Christ suffered in the flesh, and we must do so too if we are to be faithful to Him. Our lives were filled with sin, but we turned away from sin toward Christ. This is difficult for the unsaved to accept. A godly life which is changed is convicting. They will often speak evil of us or try to bring us back "into the fold" and participate in their sins. But we must not do so.

1 Peter 4:[12] Beloved, think it not strange concerning the fiery trial which is to try you, as though some strange thing happened unto you:[13] But rejoice, inasmuch as ye are partakers of Christ's sufferings; that, when his glory shall be revealed, ye may be glad also with exceeding joy.[14] If ye be reproached for the name of Christ, happy are ye; for the spirit of glory and of God resteth upon you: on their part he is evil spoken of, but on your part he is glorified.[15] But let none of you suffer as a murderer, or as a thief, or as an evildoer, or as a busybody in other men's matters.[16] Yet if any man suffer as a Christian, let him not be ashamed; but let him glorify God on this behalf.[17] For the time is come that judgment must begin at the house of God: and if it first begin at us, what shall the end be of them that obey not the gospel of God?[18] And if the righteous scarcely be saved, where shall the ungodly and the sinner appear?[19] Wherefore let them that suffer according to the will of God commit the keeping of their souls to him in well doing, as unto a faithful Creator.

We can expect fiery trials. They show that we are partakers of the sufferings of Christ. But we must be careful that we do not undergo trials because of our own sin. These tests must come because of our righteous lives, and not because of our sinful lifestyle. Then we can commit ourselves to God. He will make things come out in the right manner.

I might mention again that even when we suffer for righteousness sake, forgiveness is the key to the ultimate result. When Zacharias was stoned to death at the order of King Joas, he prayed that God would see and take revenge. And indeed, God saw, and took revenge. Joas was eventually killed. But when Stephen was stoned for witnessing to Christ, he asked for forgiveness. Even as Saul persecuted the church immediately following his death, those who ran elsewhere witnessed and the church grew. And not long afterward, Saul became the apostle Paul, perhaps the greatest example of a Christian in the New Testament.

Paul had already spoken about the purifying effects of trials. *1 Peter 1:[6] Wherein ye greatly rejoice, though now for a season, if need be, ye are in heaviness through manifold temptations:[7] That the trial of your faith, being much more precious than of gold that perisheth, though it be tried with fire, might be found unto praise and honour and glory at the appearing of Jesus Christ.* But now he adds another thought - that we are partakers in Christ's sufferings. Of course, this will only occur if we suffer for doing good, and not for doing evil, since Christ was without sin. Suffering for doing good is a mark of God's spirit resting upon us. This is no cause for shame. And we must not be shocked, because God will judge and test His own children for their worthiness to receive their inheritance. So, we must suffer according to the will of God and give our souls over to Him.

Thus, grace is seen as suffering for one's faithfulness to God. From the world's perspective, suffering and enduring is a tragedy. But God views it as grace: enduring suffering through His power. Because it is grace, it is God's work and nothing for us to boast about. This testing and grace is a present from God to us. We get this grace the moment we need it.

However, we will usually respond like we live. Let us learn obedience now. We must live as peaceably as we can and when trials come, we must trust the Lord. We are not to fear or retaliate. We must not be surprised at the fiery trial. Our suffering and faith will be noticed while on earth; but rewards may be delayed until heaven. Suffering for good is evidence of God's glorious spirit resting upon us. But we must not be proud, but rest in God's grace. Remember, the world takes offense at Christ's message, and sometimes just at the presence of His followers. We can expect persecution.

However, although we do not have to fight Satan, we must resist him. *1 Peter 5:[5] Likewise, ye younger, submit yourselves unto the elder. Yea, all of you be subject one to another, and be clothed with humility: for God resisteth the proud, and giveth grace to the humble.[6] Humble yourselves therefore under the mighty hand of God, that he may exalt you in due time:[7] Casting all your care upon him; for he careth for you.[8] Be sober, be vigilant; because your adversary the devil, as a roaring lion, walketh about, seeking whom he may devour:[9] Whom resist stedfast in the faith, knowing that the same afflictions are accomplished in your brethren that are in the world.[10] But the God of all grace, who hath called us unto his eternal glory by Christ Jesus, after that ye have suffered a while, make you perfect, stablish, strengthen, settle you.*

God promises to restore us where we have broken down. God promises to give us the backbone needed to withstand the temptation to deny him. But it is the humble who will receive the grace of God, that power which we need in times of trial. God promises to strengthen us to resist Satan even unto death. God promises to establish us and give us a firm foundation. It is through suffering that God develops the personal character of his people. Suffering never thwarts God's purposes. No suffering, no glory. This is how He gives grace in a rebellious and fallen world.

Persecution in Revelation

In the book of Revelation, we find the answer pertaining to God's revelation of Himself is the same as in the book of Job. He does not answer "why" but rather "who." Revelation reveals much about who Jesus really is. I do not believe that Job ever realized the contest between God and Satan over him while he was still living on earth. But he realized who God was and that he could trust Him.

It is a great comfort to the churches facing persecution that Jesus is God incarnate, and that He is sovereign. This incarnate Jesus walked in the midst of seven churches and knew their problems. The church at Ephesus had strict unloving orthodoxy. The church in Smyrna struggled with fear of suffering. The church at Pergamos had false doctrines creeping in. The church at Thyatira had problems with moral and ethical purity. The church in Sardis was spiritually dead. The church in Philadelphia was challenged to look for doors which were open to the gospel. And the church at Laodicea was totally worldly. Jesus is in their midst to challenge them and to provide them with victory.

In the book of Revelation, we find a cosmic struggle between Satan and the Lamb of God. The Lamb wins, but He is killed in the battle. His messengers overcome, but they win through suffering and death. Their testimony (marturia) always involves suffering and death. And Jesus was the faithful witness. *Revelation 1:[4] John to the seven churches which are in Asia: Grace be unto you, and peace, from him which is, and which was, and which is to come; and from the seven Spirits which are before his throne;[5] And from Jesus Christ, who is the faithful witness, and the first begotten of the dead, and the prince of the kings of the earth. Unto him that loved us, and washed us from our sins in his own blood,[6] And hath made us kings and priests unto God and his Father; to him be glory and dominion for ever and ever. Amen.*

The only method God uses to bring the nations to Himself is through the testimony of Jesus Christ. Jesus is the Lamb that was slain. John reports his vision in *Revelation 5:[6] And I beheld, and, lo, in the midst of the throne and of the four beasts, and in the midst of the elders, stood a Lamb as it had been slain, having seven horns and seven eyes, which are the seven Spirits of God sent forth into all the earth.[7] And he came and took the book out of the right hand of him that sat upon the throne.[8] And when he had taken the book, the four beasts and four and twenty elders fell down before the Lamb, having every one of them harps, and golden vials full of odours, which are the prayers of saints. [9] And they sung a new song, saying, Thou art worthy to take the book, and to open the seals thereof: for thou wast slain, and hast redeemed us to God by thy blood out of every kindred, and tongue, and people, and nation;[10] And hast made us unto our God kings and priests: and we shall reign on the earth.[11] And I beheld, and I heard the voice of many angels round about the throne and the beasts and the elders: and the number of them was ten thousand times ten thousand, and thousands of thousands;[12] Saying with a loud voice, Worthy is the Lamb that was slain to receive power, and riches, and wisdom, and strength, and honour, and glory, and blessing.[13] And every creature which is in heaven, and on the earth, and under the earth, and such as are in the sea, and all that are in them, heard I saying, Blessing, and honour, and glory, and power, be unto him that sitteth upon the throne, and unto the Lamb for ever and ever.[14] And the four beasts said, Amen. And the four and twenty elders fell down and worshipped him that liveth for ever and ever.* Notice the emphasis that the Lamb is worthy because He was slain — He was the faithful witness unto death.

This testimony is witnessed and propagated by faithful witnesses and sealed by their blood. *Revelation 6:[9] And when he had opened the fifth seal, I saw under the altar the souls of them that were slain for the word of God, and for the testimony which they held:[10] And they cried with a loud voice, saying, How long, O Lord, holy and true, dost thou not judge and avenge our blood on them that dwell on the earth?[11] And white robes were given unto every one of them; and it was said unto them, that they should rest yet for a little season, until their fellow servants also and their brethren, that should be killed as they were, should be fulfilled.*

Revelation 7:[9] After this I beheld, and, lo, a great multitude, which no man could number, of all nations, and kindreds, and people, and tongues, stood before the throne, and before the Lamb, clothed with white robes, and palms in their hands;[10] And cried with a loud voice, saying, Salvation to our God which sitteth upon the throne, and unto the Lamb.[11] And all the angels stood round about the throne, and about the elders and the four beasts, and fell before the throne on their faces, and worshipped God,[12] Saying, Amen: Blessing, and glory, and wisdom, and thanksgiving, and honour, and power, and might, be unto our God for ever and ever. Amen.[13] And one of the elders answered, saying unto me, What are these which are arrayed in white robes? and whence came they?[14] And I said unto him, Sir, thou knowest.

And he said to me, These are they which came out of great tribulation, and have washed their robes, and made them white in the blood of the Lamb. Thus, we see a great cloud of witnesses during the time of tribulation.

We find the same situation with the two witnesses of *Revelation 11:[3] And I will give power unto my two witnesses, and they shall prophesy a thousand two hundred and threescore days, clothed in sackcloth.[4] These are the two olive trees, and the two candlesticks standing before the God of the earth.[5] And if any man will hurt them, fire proceedeth out of their mouth, and devoureth their enemies: and if any man will hurt them, he must in this manner be killed.[6] These have power to shut heaven, that it rain not in the days of their prophecy: and have power over waters to turn them to blood, and to smite the earth with all plagues, as often as they will. [7] And when they shall have finished their testimony, the beast that ascendeth out of the bottomless pit shall make war against them, and shall overcome them, and kill them.[8] And their dead bodies shall lie in the street of the great city, which spiritually is called Sodom and Egypt, where also our Lord was crucified.[9] And they of the people and kindreds and tongues and nations shall see their dead bodies three days and an half, and shall not suffer their dead bodies to be put in graves.[10] And they that dwell upon the earth shall rejoice over them, and make merry, and shall send gifts one to another; because these two prophets tormented them that dwelt on the earth.[11] And after three days and an half the Spirit of life from God entered into them, and they stood upon their feet; and great fear fell upon them which saw them.[12] And they heard a great voice from heaven saying unto them, Come up hither. And they ascended up to heaven in a cloud; and their enemies beheld them.* Again, the followers of Jesus were witnesses who died but were resurrected, just as Jesus had died and was resurrected.

God always works consistent with His own nature. He persuades through love, although He has all authority and power.

Force is counter-productive and leads to hatred and revolt. The answer is the cross. Notice that in the same way that Christ was victorious over Satan at the cross, so His witnesses conquered Satan by the word of testimony and the blood of Christ! *Revelation 12:[11] And they overcame him by the word of their testimony; and they loved not their lives unto the death.* We find that Satan often uses the fear of death to intimidate man to follow him. But Jesus has won over death and released us from the fear of death. *Hebrews 2:[14] Forasmuch then as the children are partakers of flesh and blood, he also himself likewise took part of the same; that through death he might destroy him that had the power of death, that is, the devil;[15] And deliver them who through fear of death were all their lifetime subject to bondage.*

At the conclusion of the Book of Revelation, we find the Lamb and those who follow Him, victorious. This is, of course, a tremendous encouragement for those under persecution to persist despite the opposition. And we find that God builds a new heaven and earth where righteousness reigns, and we who are approved will have a part in ruling over the new creation.

It is important to remember the key place of the Holy Spirit in the life of the individual, especially as He is a witness. Jesus spoke extensively about the Holy Spirit the night before His crucifixion. It is the Holy Spirit who empowers the believer to speak with clarity and power. He will give the right words to say. It is the Holy Spirit who convicts and convinces the lost of their need for Christ. The believer is not alone. God the Holy Spirit is in charge of world evangelism. He is with the believer and will never leave him. He has authorized the believer to be a witness and an ambassador for Christ. He is the Comforter in trials and tribulations. And it is the Holy Spirit who transforms the believer to be what he should be.

The History of Martyrdom and Persecution from the 1st to the 21st Century

Persecution – An overview

Persecution started with Cain and Abel, and has continued to the present time. Since the time of the death and resurrection of Jesus Christ, there have been three major periods of persecution, although there is some persecution continually. Paul stated in *2 Timothy 3:12: Yea, and all that will live godly in Christ Jesus shall suffer persecution.*

The first major persecution started with religious persecution by the Jewish leadership until the time of Nero. During this time, initially Christianity was considered a protected religion as a sect of Judaism. The original church arose in Jerusalem and initially the majority of Christians came out of Judaism. However, it became apparent that the Christians were not simply an offshoot of Judaism, but a different religion, and 10 waves of persecution occurred under the Roman government until Christianity was eventually no longer persecuted in 317 and soon became the official religion of the Roman empire.

The second great wave of persecution occurred at the time of the Protestant revolution in the 16th and 17th centuries. There was, of course, some persecution over the preceding 12 centuries, but a great wave of persecution occurred especially in Europe resulting in the martyrdom of millions.

The third great wave of persecution has arisen over the last century, especially during the 20th and 21st centuries. This persecution has been worldwide and has been particularly prevalent in communist countries and in countries under Islamic domination, as well as a number of autocratic countries such as North Korea and Burma. We will outline some of the main features of the more recent history of persecution in the following pages.

Persecution of the Early Apostles and Believers

Although we do not have scripture outlining the deaths of the apostles except for James, the brother of John, we do have traditions about their deaths. Virtually all the apostles, with the exception of John, were killed as martyrs. John was boiled in oil by Domitian, but God protected him and he preached while in the oil. Then he was exiled to Patmos, where he received the revelation recorded as the last book of the New Testament, but he returned to Ephesus after the death of Domitian. James was beheaded by Herod Agrippa, who killed other Christians and imprisoned Peter (See Acts 12). The Lord sent an angel and released Peter, who was later crucified upside down by Nero. The same Nero had Paul, who was a Roman citizen, beheaded. We believe that both died following the fire which destroyed much of Rome, and was falsely attributed to Christians, probably about 67 A.D.

Phillip was scourged, imprisoned and crucified at Hieropolis in Phrygia. Matthew was killed by the sword. James the just, the half-brother of Jesus, was thrown down from the top of the temple when he refused to deny Christ. He survived but was then stoned and clubbed to death while praying for his persecutors.

Matthias was stoned and beheaded at Jerusalem. Mark was dragged to pieces by a mob in front of their idol, Serapis. Andrew was crucified with two pieces of the cross on the ground. Jude (Thaddeus) was crucified at Edessa. Bartholomew was beaten and crucified in India. Priests in India thrust lances through Thomas. Luke was hung from an olive tree. Jude was shot with arrows. Barnabas was burned at Salamis. In one catacomb in Rome, there are the bodies of 174,000 martyrs. Others were flayed alive, dragged by horses, and killed in the arena.

Reasons for Persecution Under Rome

Rome wanted a uniform world under the Roman government, and one stabilizing factor was the worship of the Emperor. The Christians placed Christ before Caesar and undermined the classic culture which Rome wanted to propagate. Furthermore, when the Christians prayed, they did not pray to idols that were visible, so they were considered atheists. When they had the "kiss of peace," they were accused of immorality. They were also accused of cannibalism because they "ate the body of Christ." The state tolerated other religions in addition to the worship of the genius of Caesar, but they must be secondary to the state, and not above the state in priority.

Furthermore, Christians undermined the aristocracy by holding that all people are equal. They lived pure lives, which were a rebuke to the lives of many pagans. They did not participate in many rites, nor in the entertainment of the masses, including the theater and the arena. By opposing the worship of idols, they threatened the economy of the idol-makers, such as those in Ephesus. Furthermore, Judaism was an accepted and protected sect, but when it became apparent that the Christians were not a part of the Jewish sect, Christianity became illegal.

There were ten major persecutions by Rome between 64 A.D. under Nero and 303 A.D. under Diocletian. The emperors, beginning with Augustus, were considered divine gods who must be worshipped. Also, Nero sought a scapegoat for the burning of Rome, and persecuted Christians, murdering many, including Peter and Paul. Domitian exiled John after failing to kill him. Furthermore, as the church gained power, it was viewed as a threat. Despite persecution, during this period the number of Christians increased to between 5-15% of the total population of the Roman Empire.

Initially, as mentioned in the book of Acts, most persecution came from the jealous Jews or unruly mobs, but official Roman persecution soon followed and existed until the time of

111

Constantine. After the persecution under Nero about 64 A.D., the next persecution was during the reign of Domitian about 90 A.D. A typical example of this period is that of Tragan in 112 A. D. In a letter to government officials, he said to not seek out Christians, but if one is brought to them, they are to ask him three times if he is a Christian. If he continues to answer positively, then kill him. A standard test was to bring the Christian before an image of the Caesar. If he would offer incense to the genius of the Caesar, he was given a certificate and freed. If he refused, he was executed. Most of the early persecution from the Roman Empire tended to be periodic. There was not much persecution from other religions or from other Christians during this time.

Ignatius, who was the bishop of Antioch, was a contemporary of the apostle John. In 107-108 A. D., he was tried, convicted of being a Christian, and condemned to be fed to lions in the arena at Rome. He was marched by foot all the way to Rome, bound with 10 chains and tied to 10 men. These chains were never removed. However, he was concerned that those in Rome would prevent him from dying a martyr's death. He felt that by dying, his testimony would be clear, but it would not be so clear if he were pardoned. He asked the Christians who might pray for him, to pray that the lions would so consume his body that nothing of him would remain. Indeed, at his death, only the harder parts of his body were not consumed. These were gathered together and returned as relics to Antioch. Ignatius felt that he was a co-laborer with God, but that the work could not be completed without suffering.[19] He felt that through the grace of God and suffering, he might obtain his inheritance.

About the same year, Phocus, the bishop of Sineppe, refused to offer incense to the idol of Neptune. He was sentenced to die and thrown first into a lime kiln and then into boiling water.[20] Somewhat later Marcus Aurelius, a Stoic emperor, believed that Christians were the cause of many of the problems of his time. He killed Justyn Martyr. In the same time period, Vitalius, a

Roman nobleman, was buried alive. His wife was discovered to be a Christian and was beaten to death with sticks.[21]

The Example of Polycarp

Polycarp was a disciple of John, and a bishop of Smyrna. His martyrdom was about 50 years after that of Ignatius. Polycarp was well known and hated by unbelievers because he spoke against idolatry. He was not only effective in Smyrna but traveled to Rome. He was known for the power of his prayers.

Ton makes a number of points about Polycarp's martyrdom, quoting from sources evaluating the early martyrs.[22] It was a time of great persecution. Polycarp did not provoke persecution of himself by turning himself in, but neither did he run away, thus enabling the authorities to find him if they so desired. He had a vision three days before his trial of a pillow bursting into flames and was convinced that he would be burned alive. Nevertheless, his focus was on the influence he might have on others, rather than focusing on himself. He was praying for others when he was captured, although he had been warned and could have escaped. He ordered that food and drink be given to those who captured him, and then he spent two full hours in prayer before accompanying them. The

There was an easy way for Polycarp to avoid torture. He simply had to offer some incense and say "Caesar is Lord." But Polycarp heard a voice from heaven tell him: "Be brave, Polycarp, and act like a man." The proconsul told Polycarp that he would be released if he would curse Christ. His answer is classic and has been quoted often. "Eighty-six years I have served Him, and He never did me any wrong. How can I blaspheme my King who saved me?" When Polycarp was threated to be killed by wild beasts, he was unafraid. Then he was threatened with burning. Polycarp in turn warned him against a fire that burned not for an hour, but the fire of eternal punishment. Polycarp went to the stake unafraid. He prayed, thanking the Lord for the privilege of dying as a martyr and asking that he be accepted as a burned offering to Christ. Apparently, the Christians gathered his bones which remained to celebrate the memory of his martyrdom and had communion on top of his grave. It was reported that the wind blew the fire away from his body and encompassed it. Eventually, the emperor ordered that he be killed by a dagger. His blood was said to put out the fire. His dead body was then placed on the fire and consumed. His bones were collected as relics and kept in Smyrna.

In contrast to Polycarp, there was mention of a man called Quintus, who turned himself in as a Christian, actually seeking martyrdom. However, when he saw the wild beasts, he shrank back in fear. He recanted when urged repeatedly by the proconsul. Another Christian, Germanicus, demonstrated steadfastness facing martyrdom, actually attracting wild beasts to himself to speed up their attack. It seems that when the Lord called someone to martyrdom, He stood by the martyr and enabled him to withstand the torture and death. Ton notices several basic points concerning this truth. It is God who marks out a person for martyrdom. It is not the person's choice. Furthermore, it is a great honor. The martyrs believed in an immediate resurrection and reward.

Justin Martyr

Justin Martyr was born in Samaria and raised in the pagan philosophies of the day. While in Rome, he saw the steadfastness of Christians while a disciple of Plato and concluded that they were honorable individuals. He founded a school of philosophy and wrote extensively. During the days of Marcus Aurelius, he was accused by a pagan philosopher and made to stand trial under Junius Rusticus, a Roman general and philosopher. At the trial, he gave a powerful testimony for Jesus Christ and refused to worship Caesar. He and other Christians who were tried with him were condemned after confessing that they were Christians and after being scourged, they were beheaded.

We have accounts of a number of other martyrs about the same time who proved to be steadfast in their faith. They refused to worship Caesar and thanked God for the privilege of suffering for His sake.

The Martyrs of Lyons

In 177 A. D., there was ferocious persecution of Christians in the area of Lyons. The Romans could not tolerate the Christians who asserted that Jesus Christ, not Caesar, is Lord. A large group of Christians were rounded up, and eventually tortured and martyred. They were given a chance to confess Caesar as Lord, and if they did not, they were tortured. Some of the Christians denied Christ under torture and confessed that the Christians did immoral activities and even participated in cannibalism. But the majority of the Christians stood firm despite incredible torture.

One of the heroes of the faith was a slave woman, Blandina, whom some of the Christians were afraid might deny the faith because she was not physically strong. She was tortured one entire day, until her tormentors finally gave up taking turns torturing her. She was made to watch the torture and death of other martyrs, but through it all, she encouraged others to endure and confess Christ. Finally, she was forced to sit in a heated iron stool, and after being severely burned, was tossed by wild bulls until she died.

Bishop Plothinus, a frail 90-year-old man, was strengthened to endure torture and die as a martyr. Sanctus was tortured horribly and died a noble death, as did the nobleman Vellitius, who had led an exemplary life. Although the usual practice was to release those who broke under torture, in Lyons they were returned to jail with those who were to be martyred. Those who had held forth, whom they called "confessors," who had not denied the faith, encouraged those who had broken under torture, and many recovered and went to the judges. The judges expected them to recant, but they confessed Christ and joined the martyrs.[23]

One who had survived this awful torture wrote of their experiences. He explained the persecution as being instigated by

Satan. Satan instigated not only the horrible torture, but also the kind words of the judges to release Christians from certain death if they would recant. The steadfast beliefs of the martyrs dealt a tremendous blow to Satan. We see again that God, in His wisdom, has used the martyrs instead of force. The author of the description also showed that the martyrs were chosen by God, and that God was with them. It was He who enabled them the supernatural strength to endure torture. The author noted that God's grace not only enabled the martyrs to endure, but also to help those who had fallen to rise up again and witness for Christ.

False Teachings Arose About the Martyrs Being Able to Forgive Sins

Unfortunately, later people began to look at this grace as the possession of the martyr (or the church, especially the Roman Catholic Church), which is a truly unscriptural doctrine. The grace was a gift given at the time of need, and not a possession of the individual to be dispensed by that individual, or to be held in reserve for the church. That was the beginning of worship of the saints

Perpetua was a young woman, the daughter of a nobleman, who had recently given birth. She had become a Christian, which was a great shame to her family, who begged her to renounce her faith. Her father underwent a beating to have her freed and pled with her to recant. Perpetua eventually pushed her family away. She was imprisoned and condemned to death. She had several visions during her imprisonment; dreaming of a golden ladder leading to heaven but blocked by the devil at the bottom. She had to smash the devil's head to proceed. In another vision, she saw her brother in hell, but she prayed for him and he went to heaven. She also saw a vision of fighting an Egyptian.

Perpetua was accompanied by a slave girl, Felicia, who also desired martyrdom. Felicia was afraid that she would not be martyred, being eight months pregnant. But with the prayers of other Christians, she delivered the infant and both were brought to the arena along with the other Christians. Perpetua was gored by a bull and eventually executed by gladiators.

Unfortunately, after learning about her visions, some began to think that God gave special power to prayers of the saints. Clement of Alexandria counteracted a movement to seek martyrdom by pointing out that some are not true martyrs, and not chosen by God, but that they are seeking their own deaths. Clement was correct in that the true martyr does not seek his own death. Death happens to him. However, what Clement did was to replace martyrdom with asceticism as another way of gaining merit.

Origen, who lived in the 3rd century, died as a martyr in 254. He was a noted theologian but did not use the grammatico-historical method to interpret the scriptures but used allegory instead. He came to the point of believing that the death of the martyrs actually had atoning value, and could forgive sins, as Jesus' blood forgave sins. He was severely tortured by Decius, and later died. Unfortunately, some of his ideas were perpetuated by the church.

About the same time, there was considerable confusion among the confessors during a persecution by Decius. There had not been persecution for some time, and apparently many Christians had sacrificed to idols, and others had bribed officials to give false certificates that they had done so to avoid persecution. However, a number of Christians were tortured for their faith and awaited execution when suddenly Decius died and they were released. Now the church had looked at confessors as martyrs even if they had not died. Could they forgive sins? Cyprian, the bishop of Carthage, wrote that there were different degrees of apostasy, but in all situations, there was a long period of penitence. He also stated that the martyrs were not really able to forgive sins.

During the reign of Decius, Cyprian went into hiding, but was captured during the persecution of Valerian a few years later.

He was examined and then placed in a lengthy exile. He was tried a second time and executed by the sword. A few days later, the proconsul Galerius Maximus who had pronounced his sentence also died.

The last severe period of persecution by the Roman empire was under the rule of Diocletian. Churches were burned and their leaders were seized and executed if they refused to sacrifice to idols. So many Christians were jailed that there was no room for regular criminals. Eusebius, (265-339) the first church historian, looked at the church as a new nation of God, opposed by Satan. He viewed the martyrs as confessors who were then "perfected." He witnessed the longest and most vicious persecution from 306-313 A.D. Unspeakable cruelty was perpetrated, but the martyrs came forth eagerly to die. The Roman Empire eagerly sought out all copies of the scriptures and destroyed most of them. This may account for the fact that it has been difficult to obtain scriptures prior to the fourth century as most had been destroyed in this persecution.

Active Persecution by the Roman Empire Ends

In 311, Galerius wrote the first edict of toleration, and persecution basically stopped. And in 313, Constantine gave freedom of religion after he had won a great military victory. Before the battle, he had seen a vision of a cross in the sky with a voice telling him to conquer in this sign. He painted crosses on the shields of his soldiers, marched them by a river where priests sprinkled them en masse to "baptize" them, and then won the battle and became emperor. Christian persecution by the Roman Empire basically stopped.

Cults of Martyrs

Now a cult of martyrs began to rise up. With the belief that the martyrs could intercede for individuals, and also that they could forgive sins, it was a short step to praying to them as saints. By the fourth and fifth centuries, saints were honored in seven ways:

1. The name of the martyr was inscribed in the catalogue of saints, and they were ordered a public recognition.

2. His/her intercession was invoked at public prayers.

3. Churches were dedicated to God in his/her memory.

4. The Eucharist and divine office were celebrated in his/her honor.

5. His/her festival was observed.

6. They made representations of him/her surrounded by divine light.

7. His/her relics were enclosed in precious vessels and publicly honored.[24]

A Christian writer named Victricius believed that the saints were in close relationship with God, and all parts of their bodies included this grace. So, any relic was helpful in producing healing. Even more surprising, both Jerome and Augustine defended this practice. Jerome believed that the saint in heaven was still praying for the church, but now with greater power. Both men tried to limit the power of the saints to their union with Christ, and not to worship but simply respect them, but such limitations were not really held. People began building churches and chapels and seeking relics. Each saint had a day and special power for certain things. They began to pray more to the saint than to God Himself. Thus, in many ways the church began to resemble the pagan religions around her.

With the development of monasticism, such men as Clement of Alexandria began to equate the monk with the martyr. Clement felt that it was not the death of the martyr that was important, but the evidence of perfect love - and that this could be demonstrated by renouncing worldliness. Origen placed other evidence of witness almost at the level of martyrdom and wanted a life of self-renunciation and total commitment to God. They began to view the monk's vows of renunciation like a second baptism. The monk's ideal was to withdraw both from the world and from the church.

One thing that is worth remembering is that Polycarp showed that the martyr does not choose or provoke his martyrdom. It is permitted by God. But the monk is choosing to renounce the world and make his vows and promises. It is self-provoked and self-inflicted. If indeed God has chosen martyrdom for the martyr, God will enable the martyr to withstand and provide a good witness. Jesus showed that martyrdom comes when one preaches the gospel to a hostile people. On the other hand, the monk that runs to the desert is running away from the command of Christ to witness to the lost.

During the Middle Ages, the saints increased in number, and legends abounded about their power. They dominated the lives of many of the common people, who would go on pilgrimages and worship relics. Later, during the reformation, the Protestants sought to demolish the entire superstructure, and see instead the providence of God in life, and the mediation of Jesus Christ, without any human mediators. During this period, the church began to practice more and more aberrant doctrines, such as baptismal regeneration, infant baptism, the worship of Mary and the saints, and the doctrine of transubstantiation. These false doctrines allowed the dominant Roman Catholic church to increase her economic and political dominance, especially in Europe. A number of conferences of the church established these doctrinal errors, and allowed the traditions of the church to have equal authority as the scriptures, even when the rulings actually conflicted with Biblical teaching.

Throughout the middle ages there were several groups of believers who attempted to return to the original beliefs of the Bible. Among them were Donatists, Paterines, Cathari, Paulicians, and Ana Baptists; and a little later, Petro-Brussians, Arnoldists, Henricians, Albigenses, and Waldenses. Sometimes one group of these was the most prominent and sometimes another. But some of them were almost always present despite the persistency and terribleness of their persecution. (See Carroll,

J. M.. The Trail of Blood: Following the Christians down through the centuries -- or, The history of Baptist churches from the time of Christ, their founder, to the present day (p. 22). www.bibleschool.edu. Kindle Edition.)

It has been difficult to get accurate information concerning these various groups. They did not leave a substantial record of their beliefs and practices, and their enemies often distorted the facts concerning them. Furthermore, they were often denied access to the Bibles available at that time, which were usually in Latin and limited to those in formal training as clergy in the Roman Catholic church.

Persecution During the Reformation

One of the earliest reformers was John Wycliffe (1320-1384). He opposed a number of the aberrant doctrines of the Roman Catholic Church, including transubstantiation. He was perhaps the first man to translate the Bible into the English language, using the Latin Vulgate as his base. The translation was later completed by Nicholas of Hereford. Wycliffe's influence was greatly increased because of his training of the friars (Lollards) who taught the people in their own native language. The church authorities were furious at his teaching. He died of a stroke; nevertheless, his body was exhumed, burned, and then the ashes thrown into the River Swift. He was condemned as a heretic and his books burned.

In addition to his influence on the Lollards, and he had an impact in Bohemia on John Huss (1373-1415). Huss was an effective preacher and gathered believers together. He was guaranteed safe conduct to appear before the pope. However, he was condemned as a heretic and burned at the stake. When Hus challenged his persecutors, they claimed that he was a heretic, and therefore they were no longer bound by their promise of safe conduct. His followers, the United Brethren, continue to exist today. In Suriname, the EBG (Evangelical Broeders Gemeente, which translated means the evangelical brothers church), who have been continuously present since the first half of the 18th century, trace their origin to John Huss.

Savonorola (1452-1498) was another priest seeking reform. He was a fiery preacher and believed in holy living. At one point, he actually ruled the city of Florence, making extremely strict rules for governing the city which many resented. Opposition to his policies grew, and he was condemned and burned as a heretic.

Martin Luther was a potential candidate for martyrdom from the moment he challenged the Roman Catholic Church on the subject of indulgences. Luther instigated the Protestant Reformation when he nailed his 95 theses on the door of the Wittenberg Church in 1517. He was moved by the death of two Protestant martyrs from Holland and viewed this as evidence of the maturity of the church there. As he left the Diet of Worms, he was "captured" by a friend for his own protection. He translated the Bible into German. Luther opposed the Roman Catholic Church and eventually left the church, married, and began the Lutheran Church.

Luther felt that there were special privileges for those considered worthy of martyrdom. He recognized that there was a constant fight with Satan and believed that the fact that the world hated martyrs was a sign that they were genuine Christians. As the Christian is united with Christ, he is fighting against Satan. In suffering, he becomes like his Savior. God is sovereign and is using the attacks of Satan against His people for His purpose to further His church. Satanic attacks cannot be victorious, because God is ultimately Lord of all. Luther saw the purifying effects of persecution. Persecution was fertilizing the ground and trimming away dead branches and excessive foliage to make more fruit. Loss of health and possessions are simply offerings to Christ.

William Tyndale (1494-1536) was another reformer who basically accepted reformed theology. He was a brilliant linguist, fluent in eight languages, and it was claimed that he spoke each so well that you would think that it was his mother language. He translated the English Bible, not from the Vulgate, but from the original Hebrew and Greek, and his translation was so excellent that it was used as the base for several later translations. When persecution broke out, he escaped and hid in Europe. He was finally betrayed, placed in a miserable prison, and burned as a heretic. While being burned at the stake, he cried out a prayer for the Lord to open the eyes of the King of England. The Lord answered his prayer and within a very few years, a translation of the Bible in English was chained to the pulpits of the churches in England.

Other reformers arose – John Calvin and John Knox were also fervent reformers, along with Ulrich Zwingli. All three reformers rejected some of the doctrines and traditions of the Roman Catholic church. These reformers pushed forward the Reformed Church movement, but maintained a state church and infant baptism.

Persecution in England During the 16th and 17th Centuries

John Foxe lived through the time of the Protestant revolution in England under Henry VIII, Edward VI, the persecution during the reign of "bloody Mary," who attempted to return the church back to Roman Catholicism, and finally under Elizabeth I. Mary killed 275 persons for their faith during her five-year reign, including the leaders Latimer, Ridley and Cranmer. It is ironic that Latimer and Ridley had persecuted the Anabaptists before they themselves were persecuted and executed. During the reign of Mary, Foxe fled to Europe, and returned to write his famous book,[25] which later was ordered to be placed close to the Bible in every church.

Foxe felt that the battle was being fought at three levels. First, there was a battle between Christ and Antichrist. Secondly, there was a battle between the church and the world. Thirdly, there was a battle between the true church (reformed) and the false church (Catholic).

In this battle, the task of those who have found the truth was to proclaim it to the false church who needed their witness to the truth similar to the need of the heathen in the first centuries. They were willing to base their faith on the Bible and seal their testimony with their blood. Jesus, who is the Truth, had chosen them as His witnesses, and enabled them to withstand tortures otherwise impossible for humans to withstand. Many approached martyrdom with joy. They asked not for release, but for fortitude and endurance under torture and death. Many kissed the stake to which they were bound, seeing in it the cross of Christ. They were looking for a heavenly reward.

Ton states the following summary of Foxe:

> *Foxe was aware that all of human history is in fact a fierce war, a war between the people of God and the forces of hell let loose against them. God is fighting this war through His elect, through their suffering and sacrifice and death. At the same time, in the course of this war, God is testing His children, and by their endurance and faithfulness in suffering, they are showing themselves qualified for ruling with Christ in glory. The evil ones are also being tested and proven worthy of damnation.*[26]

England witnessed great persecution, especially during the turbulent times following the death of Henry VIII. Following the death of Edward VI, a protestant, and the brief reign of Lady Jane Gray, a true evangelical believer, Mary, Queen of Scots, killed many believers including Bishops Cranmer, Ridley and Latimer. She was finally beheaded after five years, and Queen Elizabeth I began her reign as the head of the Anglican church. Many died as martyrs during her reign, and many fled to Holland and to the New World, especially the Puritans.

The Roman Catholic church suffered a great loss of church members during the 16th century, especially in northern Europe.

She had attempted to reverse these losses by reforms within the church, particularly in the area of immorality among the priests and higher leadership, extending even to the popes. They attempted to control the misuse of indulgences, which were promoted as a method of extracting money from the faithful to shorten the time in purgatory of those who had died. The council of Trent was also held for a number of years during the mid-sixteenth century. Their pronouncements basically labeled all the protestant doctrines, especially salvation by faith alone without works, and the Bible as the source of doctrine without the traditions of the church, as anathema (the curse of God). The Roman Catholic church became at this point, if not earlier, clearly apostate.

Two methods which the Roman Catholics used against any protestant group were the ban and the inquisition. The inquisition was incredibly cruel torture used both to extract information from individuals and force them to recant and accept the Catholic doctrines. Many were tortured, which included on many occasions that individuals would be executed b cruel deaths such as being burned at the stake, drowned, strangled, or even drawn and quartered.

The second method of hindering conversion was the ban. Many books were forbidden, including any books which were written by Protestants. For example, Martin Luther was confronted about his writings, as were many other Protestant leaders. Included in the list of forbidden books was any translation of the Bible into the vernacular language of the people. Thus, the translations of Wycliffe, Tyndale, Luther and others were banned and precipitated Tyndale's death and the condemnation of Wycliffe. Although the claim was made that it was not safe to have uneducated individuals reading the Word of God in their own language, if they could have them available, the difference between the Roman Catholic practices and the Bible would become glaringly apparent.

Persecution of Anabaptists

One group was persecuted by all other Christian groups - the Anabaptists. They were persecuted by the Roman Catholics, but also by the Protestant churches – Lutheran, Presbyterian, and Anglican. The prevailing belief at the time was that of the state church. The state would decide which faith all of the subjects of that state would accept. Infant baptism into the state church would provide uniformity and guarantee that all subjects were of the same religion. This would, of course, produce a mixture of saved believers and unsaved unbelievers, and one could predict that the unbelievers would eventually dominate. (Think of Jesus' statement in the Sermon on the Mount that we must enter by the narrow gate where few persons walk (Matthew 7:13-14).

The more radical reformers did not want to simply reform some of the more obvious faults of the Roman Catholic church, but to return to the original apostolic model of the church. They realized while studying the scriptures that baptism was to be performed only on believers. The first Anabaptists near Zurich were re-baptized by immersion after the leader had baptized himself. One of the key reformers, Ulrich Zwingli, who ruled Geneva, was originally sympathetic to the Anabaptist doctrine. He later changed his mind and persecuted them viciously. His friend Hubmaier was put on the rack and later executed. Zwingli put a group of 20 persons, including women and children, in a dungeon with inadequate food until they had all perished together.

The Anabaptist groups were viciously persecuted for approximately 150 years. They were persecuted by the Catholics initially, but later also by the Lutherans, the Reformed (Calvinists), the Anglicans, and eventually by the Congregationalists in the New World. They were tortured, drowned, beheaded, and burned at the stake, and yet they persisted. At one place in Europe, there was a road with stakes placed every few feet, and on each stake, the severed head of an Anabaptist. It is estimated that perhaps 50,000,000 died during the dark ages and the beginning of the reformation.[27]

There were other groups which were persecuted as well. France persecuted the Hugenots until they were essentially wiped out, especially after the infamous St. Bartholomew Day massacre.[28] Men, women and children were hunted and killed. Likewise, a colony which was started in Brazil was betrayed and its members were killed. As mentioned above, the Catholics used particularly the inquisition and the ban. Under the ban, it was illegal to read protestant literature. And through the inquisition, many persons renounced their faith under torture. An estimated 10,000 died for their faith. The Catholics did lose substantial areas of northern Europe, but were able to maintain their presence in Portugal, Spain, France, and most of southern Europe. They expanded their number by annexing many territories found by explorers, especially in the New World.

The Anabaptists were called by different names, often named after the founder of their particular group, such as the Hutterites (Jacob Hutter) or the Mennonites (Menno Simons). They believed in baptism following a personal encounter with Jesus Christ. They expected a visible transformation of the individual's life, obedience to the Lord's commands, and they expected imitation of the Lord in all areas, including suffering.

The Anabaptists looked at suffering for Christ as both a means of purifying and transforming the Christian through suffering, and also a test of the genuineness of his faith. Baptism and communion were considered suffering. Baptism was viewed as a sacrifice because the Lord used it figuratively, speaking of His forthcoming sacrificial death, but it was also an oath of discipleship, and a promise to follow Christ wherever He went. At that time, any adult who underwent baptism was to be prepared to die, but it was more than death to self and death to the world; often it meant death by torture or the stake or the sword. In the same way, when they took part in communion, they emphasized the bread, which represented unity in the believers, as it was first grain that was crushed and then baked together.

Likewise, the cup symbolized individual grapes which were crushed together and then drunk.

The Anabaptists also saw the world as two kingdoms - the kingdom of this world and the kingdom of God. Both kingdoms had different rulers and different rules. Each individual must decide which kingdom to join. The kingdom of God is inevitably victorious but requires the suffering and death of many of its participants. Furthermore, there are two churches, one of God, and one of Satan. What do they fight for? The kingdom of God fights for the Truth. But Satan tricked mankind with the lie, and his kingdom is the kingdom of falsehood and darkness. The world rejects the truth, and it rejects the light. However, when the world observes self-sacrifice, it can begin to perceive the truth because the truth is consistent with itself. The world tries to eliminate and crush the truth by killing the messenger of the truth. Martyrdom manifests the truth.

The public, witnessing the boldness of the martyrs, and being aware of their pure lives, were often brought to reflect on their teaching, and ultimately to come to salvation. One official lamented that the more Anabaptists he killed, the more were raised up. The Anabaptists assembled many scriptures speaking of future rewards, meditated on them and memorized them. Even in prison, as they wrote their last letters to loved ones, they were often filled with scripture. Many of the hymns of the Anabaptists were martyr's hymns, sometimes composed as they awaited death. The Anabaptists trained their members for martyrdom and to be strong Christians. But are we in the west training ourselves in any form of sacrifice for Jesus Christ?

We do have considerable information on the Anabaptist beliefs and attitudes toward persecution. The author of Martyrs' Mirror, a huge book on persecution, was written by a Dutch author and was brought to the New World. The book outlined much persecution after the time of the apostles but has a great deal of information on persecution especially in Holland during the 17th century. Unfortunately, the movement became extreme and many unbiblical practices occurred within some groups including multiple wives and setting up independent cities such as Munster. Although Mennonites are still present in the USA and Canada, many have left the movement and the groups have separated in many cases.

Persecution in the New World

It seems strange that the same persons who came to the New World to escape religious persecution would persecute other Christians; strange but true. The first Pilgrims and other settlers in what is now America also set up their state churches and persecuted others. The Puritans, Anglicans, Congregationalists, and Presbyterians persecuted other groups when they were the official church, and they especially persecuted the Baptists. Persecution included taxation, loss of property, whipping, and incarceration.

Roger Williams developed strong separatist and Baptist ideas. When he found out that he was about to be arrested, he walked 100 miles in the dead of winter, and was rescued by Indians. Later he went to England with John Clarke to get a charter for a new colony. Williams returned to the New World, but John Clarke remained to petition the government in England. Twelve years after they attempted to get a charter from Oliver Cromwell, Rhode Island was officially chartered as the first colony with complete religious freedom, and apparently the first territory with complete religious freedom in the world. Clarke had started the first Baptist church in 1638 and the charter of the colony was in 1663.

Clarke and a visiting preacher went with Obadiah Holmes, a former Congregationalist turned Baptist, to visit a parishioner just inside the boundary of Massachusetts Bay. They were arrested, their hands were tied behind their backs, and they were marched into a Congregational church. Then they charged them with failure to remove their hats during a religious service. (Of course, they could not as their hands were tied.) They were fined, but Obadiah Holmes refused to pay the fine. He was whipped so severely that blood overflowed his boots, and he was unable to lie on his back for weeks.

Another situation arose in a small group of five Baptist families who had struggled to build a fort to survive against Indian attacks. They were taxed to build a Presbyterian church although there were no Presbyterians in their town. When they were not able to pay, their properties were sold at 10% of their value, and most of them bought by the Presbyterian minister who planned to move there.

There was even more severe persecution by the Anglicans, especially in Virginia. A young preacher, James Ireland, was arrested for preaching without the permission from the bishop. He was placed in the Culpepper local jail. He was brutally abused as they tried to kill him with sulfur fumes, and also to blow him up with gunpowder. Then they bribed a doctor to poison him. When people gathered to hear him preach, they cursed and rode horses through the crowd which had gathered to hear him. But people were saved. Eventually, after his release, a small church was built on the site of the infamous jail.

A wide variety of persecutions were endured by preachers. The actual court records include such items as the following: ducked and nearly drowned by 20 men; jailed for permitting a man to pray; meeting broken up by a mob; pulled down and hauled by the hair, shot with a shotgun, severely beaten with a whip; whipped severely by the sheriff, hands slashed while preaching. When three Baptist preachers were jailed, Patrick Henry successfully defended them. The state set a rule that only one Baptist preacher was permitted per county. He was only permitted to preach once every two months, at one location, and never at night. He was not permitted to do mission work. The government was convinced that no church could survive without government support and therefore supported the concept of the state church. Finally, in 1786, religious freedom was obtained.

When the Constitution of the United States of America was formulated, there was considerable opposition from some of the colonies to ratify it. Virginia was the strongest of the colonies, and by this time, the Baptists had considerable influence in the state. Without their support, it seemed unlikely that the Constitution would be ratified. Thomas Jefferson approached John Leland, a leading pastor of the Baptists, who agreed to support the Constitution if it would be amended with a guarantee of Freedom of Religion. Indeed, the Bill of Rights guaranteed this right as the first of the amendments, and the Constitution was ratified.

Persecution Among Foreign Missionaries

Persecution was also experienced by missionaries going to foreign lands. One of the early missionaries to die at the hands of Muslims was Raymond Lull, who tried to reach them. After his conversion, he left a profligate lifestyle, provided for his wife and children, and became a monk. He learned Arabic and wrote extensively and became a missionary to the Muslims. He had numerous conflicts with them, attacking Muhammad and promoting Christ. He was eventually stoned to death at age 80.

During the 19th century, there were many missionary martyrs reaching the South Sea Islands. John Williams and James Chalmers were killed and eaten by cannibals. John Coleridge Patteson, a brilliant Anglican bishop of Melanesia, was killed in retaliation for Europeans capturing slaves. John Paton suffered a great deal but survived and had a great ministry at Aniwa. John Thomas likewise had an effective ministry, as did Hiram Bingham and Henry Nott.

Africa was a very fruitful field but fertilized with the death of many martyrs. Some famous names of those laboring there include David Livingstone, Robert Moffat, Alexander MacKay and some dying at the hands of natives such as Bishop Hannington, but more dying from malaria and other tropical illnesses. It was said that there was a time when there were more graves of missionaries than that of converts. Missionaries would arrive with their trunks shaped big enough to serve as a coffin. Yet the harvest has been incredible. A number of sub-Sahara countries have experienced more than 50% of the native population converting from animism to Christianity.

China, India, and Southeast Asia had many famous missionaries as well. William Carey and his co-workers labored with the biggest opposition being the East India Company, who believed that missionaries interfered with profits. Hudson Taylor and Jonathan Goforth in China also had persecution during the latter portion of the 19th century. However, the results of missionary efforts in Asia have been disappointing with except for Korea, the Philippine Islands, and more recently, the revival in China over the last 30-40 years.

As we move to the 20th century, we find many more missionaries martyred. Five New Tribes missionaries were killed in the 1940's in Bolivia by hostile Indians. In 1955, five missionaries from three missions tried to reach the Auca Indians. Two of them were especially well known: Jim Elliot and Nate Saint. All five were killed. Later Elliot's wife and Nate Saint's sister lived with the tribe for many years and many of the members came to Christ. Chet Bitterson, a young linguist under Wycliffe Bible Translators, was executed by Marxist rebels in Columbia. Initially Latin America was nominally Catholic. However, since the second world war, the Pentecostal movement has dominated in Latin America.

In Africa, Dr. Carl Becker, a medical doctor and expert in leprosy, was chased out of Belgian Congo by the Simbas. Others were not as fortunate. Dr. Helen Roseveare was captured and raped repeatedly. Dr. Paul Carlson was shot to death during a rescue attempt by Belgian troops. Hector McMillan was killed, but his two boys survived by playing dead. His twelve year old son prayed as Jesus had prayed from the cross: "Father forgive them, for they know not what they do." Jay Tucker was tortured and killed with broken bottles and his blood-covered dead body was dumped in a nearby river to be consumed by crocodiles. He and his wife had prayed for the salvation of a tribe very resistant to the gospel. That tribe had a tradition that someone whose blood flowed in the river would bring them the truth. One of the men Tucker had trained preached the gospel, mentioning that Tucker's blood had indeed flowed in the river. Many other missionaries were killed by natives or died of malaria or other tropical diseases. Many buried loved ones shortly after arrival on the field.

In China, 184 missionaries were killed during the Boxer Rebellion. Evangelist Jonathan Goforth was wounded during an attack, but was able to escape with his family and travel 1000 miles to safety. Later, John and Betty Stam were executed by the communists prior to World War II. More recently, Graham Staines and two sons were burned to death by radical Hindus.

For every missionary killed, there are many nationals who have been martyred for their faith. We often focus on the American or European missionaries, but many faithful converts have died as martyrs, and many more have endured persecution and remained faithful.

Worldwide Persecution Now

I will conclude with a brief summary of some of the persecution going on throughout the world at this time. It will be impossible to cover the persecution in any sort of detail. However, it is worth re-emphasizing what I mentioned above. This is the time of the third great wave of persecution. More than 80% of all persecution is directed against Christians. We saw that the first great wave of persecution was promulgated primarily by the Roman government during the first three centuries. The Roman government looked at Christianity as competition for the loyalty of its subjects. The second great wave of persecution was during the 16th and 17th centuries when the Protestant reformation occurred. The greatest persecutors were the state churches - first and foremost, the Roman Catholic

Church, but also the various state churches, especially the Lutherans and the Anglicans. We noted that all groups persecuted the Baptists. This current persecution is primarily promulgated by Communism and Islam, with radical Hinduism and Buddhism persecuting as well.

In Communist countries such as China, Vietnam, and Cuba, there is destruction of churches, imprisonment, and torture of believers. Pastors are especially targeted. North Korea, with its religion of Juche, is perhaps the most intolerant. The Muslim countries where Islam is dominant are also very intolerant. Perhaps the most intolerant is Saudi Arabia, followed by Pakistan, Afghanistan, Iran, Iraq, and Indonesia. There have been many riots and deaths also in African countries which are partially Islamic and partially Christian, especially in northern Nigeria and in Southern Sudan. Radical Hinduism with such groups as the RSS in India and Nepal has attacked Christians. Buddhists attack Christians in Sri Lanka and Southeastern Asia. Other locations include Chiapas, Mexico, where those in power have a combination of Roman Catholicism and local pagan worship. In Columbia, Marxist radical groups target Christian pastors because they dissuade the people against their form of Marxism.

Most of the information on persecution focuses on the extreme forms of persecution, including torture and martyrdom. But for every martyr, there are hundreds of believers who simply endure persecution, often for years. We hear of God's miraculous deliverance, but we need to hear also about God's sustaining power to countless believers who endure loss of opportunity or income, being despised and rejected. We need to realize that all who will live godly will suffer persecution of one form or another. Furthermore, we in the West need great wisdom when reaching out to help the persecuted, that we actually help them rather than hurt them with our efforts.

Although martyrs are in the minority, they provide a spiritual shock to our own lives. First, they demonstrate that our world is an unsafe place truly under the "god of this world," Satan. Second, they show us that some things are worth dying for – the Lord Jesus Christ and His kingdom. They challenge us to examine our own commitment to the Lord. For example, a Roman group of soldiers were committed Christians but also loyal to Caesar. They were willing to die for Caesar, but not to acknowledge him as Lord. They were condemned to die by exposure and were placed with only the scantiest clothing on a frozen lake. On the shore was a roaring fire to warm up and blankets. They simply had to walk to the fire to show their willingness to worship Caesar. Finally, one of the men broke, and ran to shore. As he did so, a Roman soldier on the shore stripped of his armor and outside clothing and dashed out onto the lake, joining the men who were freezing to death.

What are some of the causes of persecution?

There are a number of common causes resulting in persecution. I will outline a few causes mentioned by Ronald Boyd-Macmillan in his book Faith that Endures:

1. Ideological persecution, such as communism: The communists are convinced that they are correct. If you disagree, since they are in power, they will convince you by "re-education" until you agree and submit.

2. Governmental persecution: This occurs especially in totalitarian governments, who are fearful of allowing any disagreement with them. They view any deviations as a threat to their power. They want total control and view any form of independence with suspicion.

3. Family persecution: This is especially prominent in shame cultures as exist in the Mideast and Far eastern lands. The individual who becomes a Christian often brings great shame to the family. The family may retaliate by dispossessing the individual or even with "honor killing." It is not limited to becoming a Christian, although in Muslim countries this is considered apostasy, which may carry the death penalty. Women who become

pregnant out of wedlock, or marry a non-Muslim against the family wishes, or behave in ways considered immoral may also be killed. Another situation is where the family (usually in an animistic culture) believes spirit-worship must be performed by all members of the family. If one fails to do so, then the spirits may retaliate on the family. Thereby there is pressure on all the family to participate.

4. Persecution from the culture: Perhaps the best example is that of animistic spirit worship as mentioned above. The spirits may not just trouble a single family, but the entire village.

5. Persecution arising within the church itself: Occasionally members within the church will retaliate against other church members and persecute them for their own ends.

6. Persecution from corrupt individuals: Warlords and leaders of various cartels will oppose believers because they oppose the profit-making of drugs. In Chiapas, the local leaders make profit from selling liquor during their feasts and celebrations. They have persecuted Christians who refused to participate and fund their work. Paul ran into a similar situation in Ephesus. His preaching was so effective that the local silversmiths could not find buyers for their idols and ended up persecuting him.

7. The author also mentioned a situation where outside Christians came to China and would place tracts and Bibles in public areas without the knowledge or support of the local churches. The officials felt that they must do something, so they punished the local church members although they were not involved.

Sources of persecution:

As we look at the above list, we can see recurring themes of the source of persecution.

1. Islamic extremism: Islamic countries dominate the list of nations with persecution. Islam has been aggressive toward other beliefs and is especially intolerant of

Christianity and Judaism since its founding. Since the end of colonialism as a dominant force following World War II, Islam has moved toward world domination. Except for North Korea, the Open Doors list of persecuting countries are virtually all Muslim countries in the top 10 countries. After World War I, Islam suffered an embarrassing defeat, and the Ottoman Empire was divided up among victorious European nations. In recent years, fueled by finances from Petro-dollars, Islam has risen in power in many of the former European colonies. Their influence is expanding rapidly, especially in Europe.

2. Religious nationalism: Even excluding Islam, this is another dominant feature of persecution, especially with Hinduism and Buddhism. The emergence of the BJP party in India has coupled Hindutva philosophy (India is for Hindus only) with the dominant political party, making more persecution of minorities occur. In Sri Lanka, some will say that if you are not Buddhist, you are not Sri Lankan.

3. Insecurity of totalitarian governments: This is most prominent in former Communist countries, but also in such countries as Myanmar, which has been ruled by a military junta. These countries are very suspicious of any organization, including religion, which is independent of their direct observation and control. Communist China has observation of her people continually. There are also dictatorships in Africa, and most prominently in North Korea. In North Korea, if you are caught with a Bible or praying to the Christian God, not only are you arrested, but three generations of your family. Most often they disappear into a gruesome prison camp where most persons are worked so hard and fed so little that the prisoners die from starvation.

4. Secular intolerance: This type of persecution is the one most commonly experienced in the West. I have experienced a bit of this attitude while in the university

137

teaching system. When we discussed psychiatric patients, if they read a Bible, this was considered evidence of their psychiatric problem. Christians are often ridiculed, and may be removed from their employment. Academic advancement may be difficult. Many challenges meet the Christian such as abortion, accepting the truth of the Bible, transgender agenda, dealing with homosexuality, and other issues in focus today.

Countries Which Are Prominent in Persecuting Christians

Afghanistan is 98% Muslim, with only 0.02% Christians. Of the 50 languages present, only 2 have New Testament translations and three have only portions of scripture. There are no church buildings in the country. The Taliban and other radical Muslim groups persecute Christians, and they arrest and sometimes execute international aid workers. For about 20 years the United States has had a military presence in Afghanistan but made a rather abrupt withdrawal in 2021. The Taliban is reasserting its power and there are many reports of their retaliation against those who opposed their Muslim agenda.

Bangladesh, formerly part of Pakistan, has 86% Muslim, 12% Hindu, and 0.7% Christians. There are often violent acts by Muslims and Hindus. They often deny Christians access to water wells, beat them, and force them out of their homes. Some Christians are martyred.

Buddhists are very intolerant in some areas of southeast Asia, especially in Sri Lanka. Despite the promotion of Buddhism as a peaceful religion, in areas where it dominates, radical monks may lead mob violence against minorities, especially Christians. They may claim that to be a true Sri Laenkan means that you are Buddhist. The native tribes in the mountains of Southeast Asia are also often targeted.

China, the world's most populous country, has 50% listed as "nonreligious," 29% as traditional Chinese religion, and 7.2%

Christian. More Christians are imprisoned in China than in any other country. It is common to have confiscation of property and Christian materials. Churches may be bulldozed. Although a state-controlled church, and this so-called three-self church is officially recognized, the pastors cannot preach the gospel or any doctrine conflicting with communism. Therefore, 90% of all Chinese Christians belong to illegal house churches and are viewed as a threat to the communist government. They frequently undergo great persecution, especially from communist officials. At the end of World War II, the Communist Party strenuously persecuted the church, driving out missionaries and imprisoning or executing national pastors. The underground church exploded in growth. For a time, the underground church was tolerated although not accepted. In recent years, the government is cracking down on the churches again, especially those who are large and considered a threat to the power of the communist party. The growth of the church in China is one of the greatest revivals in the history of the church. One of the great needs is well-trained pastors and leaders to care for the great number of believers.

Columbia is an exception in that it is a Christian nation, with 95.5% listed as Christian, and 2.72% as nonreligious. However, there are many violent Marxist guerilla groups, especially FARC, who fund their activities with drug-related money. They destroy churches, kidnap and execute pastors, and close schools because they believe that the churches oppose their Marxist ideals and discourage the indigenous people from growing poppy and participating in the drug trade which funds their operations.

India is the world's second most populous country, and it is expected to overtake China's population soon. The population is 80% Hindu, 12.5% Muslim, and about 2.4% Christian. The country is incredibly diverse, with over 4000 different languages. There is considerable violence in a number of states, especially Orissa in northern India, where many are converted, especially from the "untouchable" class. Many churches are burned, and pastors and evangelists are murdered. The dominant party, the BJP, along with the radical RSS, use "forced conversion" as a cover for their violent activity. The Indian government has outlawed the caste system, but in practical terms, the caste system still exists. Christianity has especially reached to the lowest group, the Dalits, or untouchables. Often the lives of the Dalits improve after conversion. Forced conversion is claimed if someone improves their financial status, and often social pressure is placed on the Dalits to revert to Hinduism. Since 70% of the population is lower caste, they prop up the economy with cheap labor, and to see many of them leave caste would create a major change in the economic system.

Indonesia is the world's most populous Muslim country. It consists of 18,000 islands, of which about 6000 are populated. The population is 80.3% Muslim and 16% Christian, and there was a real revival of Christianity a number of years ago. Radical groups such as Laskar Jihad are proceeding with military actions and killings as they attempt to remove all Christians from Indonesia. They are particularly strong in some of the more remote areas where government control and support is minimal.

Iran is 99% Muslim, with a small Armenian population still remaining. The Armenians can only preach in Armenian, and not in the national language Farsi. It is illegal to witness openly. The government sends spies into congregations. The official state religion is the Shi'a form of Islam. However, despite persecution and the high risk of conversion, which may carry the death penalty for apostasy, Christianity is growing rapidly. Some believe that the Iranian church may be the fastest growing church in the world today, although the total number of Christians is still small. Such rapid growth is likely to result in increased persecution.

In northern Nigeria, 12 states have implemented Sharia law. The country is divided with approximately the same number of Christians and Muslims. The Muslims dominate the north. They have had numerous riots killing many Christians, burning homes and destroying churches. Often a pretext is given such as "insulting the Muslim faith" or "desecrating the Qur'an." In recent years, the violence has become so severe that Nigeria is now one of the top countries in the world which martyrs Christians.

North Korea is perhaps the most dangerous country to Christians in the entire world. Those found to be Christians are often killed. The percentage of the population whose religious affiliation is "nonreligious" is 64%, traditional ethnic is 16%, and Christian is estimated at 1.7%. The official doctrine is Juche, which deifies the family of Kim II Sung. Persons may be executed for such crimes as possessing a portion of the Word of God. North Korean Christians found escaping to China are usually returned and can expect execution or a slower death in a gulag where they are systematically starved, tortured, and worked to death. There are many thousands imprisoned in death camps throughout the country. The total number of Christians is unknown as it is so dangerous to witness. Some who have accepted Christ have later found out that other members of their family, even living in the same home, are truly Christian but have been afraid to share their faith because of the chance of death, not just personally, but often for three generations within the family.

Pakistan is 96% Muslim and 2.3% Christian. Militant Muslims have committed many violent acts against Christians, including rape and murder. Honor killings are not uncommon for those who have apostatized to Christianity.

Saudi Arabia is the home of Wahabi Muslim faith, which represents 92.8% of the population. They want no Christian overt activity on the entire Saudi peninsula, which they consider holy. Christians are about 4.5%. Any form of witness or Bible studies (even private in homes) can lead to incarceration, expulsion from the country, or execution. There is no church activity in Saudi Arabia.

The Communists have proven extremely cruel in their persecution.[29] Many Christians have had their fingernails pulled out, one by one. In one location, mothers and children who were Christians were arrested. When the mothers failed to recant, the children were hung. Then the adults were killed by a steamroller. To make it more painful, the steamroller ran over the feet first toward the head. These believers sang praise to the Lord in Chinese to the hymn, "More Love to Thee." One preacher was badly beaten. Then he and a number of common criminals were placed in a room filled with human waste. The prisoners were told that they would be held there indefinitely until the pastor recanted, and they took turns beating him. However, he did not recant.

Sometimes God intervenes in dramatic ways. One Orthodox priest was led away to be executed. He asked to pray before his execution and suddenly disappeared from sight. His executioners panicked. An hour later he reappeared, still on his knees, surrounded by a cloud. He was then executed. In another situation, a prisoner was cast into a pit with vicious dogs. He fell to his knees in prayer, and the dogs left him in panic, trying to escape from the pit. Some prisoners, of course, folded under the pressure, but many were enabled to endure incredible persecutions.

Methods of persecution:

In the book Faith that Endures, we find a recurring pattern used to persecute believers: a vacuum, a villain, a lie, a mob, and a megaphone. The author outlines the pattern illustrated in India, but occurring repeatedly in many different situations. I will briefly summarize his observations.

1. The vacuum: There is a problem, and the moderates fail to step up and solve the problem. After a time, people allow extremists to come up with a solution. I can think of the situation in Germany before World War II when the country was in chaos and seemed unable to solve its problems. Hitler arose to fill the vacuum.

2. A villain: There needed to be someone or some group to organize the opposition. This was then Hitler and the Nazi party. They also portrayed the Jews as a focal cause of problems.

3. The lie: Lies need to be carefully constructed to draw attention away from what may be the real causes and focus them on issues that cannot be specifically refuted. The lie can be blatantly false. But it needs to give an excuse for violence, and to create an urgency so that change cannot be avoided.

4. The mob: The mob is usually not spontaneous. It is carefully constructed and orchestrated to create chaos to intimidate the opposition. They are equipped with instructions as to what to do, and the equipment to carry out the destruction.

5. The megaphone: It is important to repeat the lie many, many times. If possible, so dominate the media and communication that it is impossible to hear anything else.

We must not think that these techniques are limited to other countries or unsophisticated people. The author outlined in detail how the opposition was able to get into power in India. At the time of the rise of Hitler, Germany was one of the most developed countries in the world but struggling with many problems when the Nazis rose to power. I believe that we are seeing many of the same techniques here in the United States in recent history.

What Are the Results of Persecution?

When I first read about revivals being tied to persecution, I thought that persecution of the church would automatically guarantee church growth. However, that is not the case. As you will see below, in some areas, persecution has led to explosive growth of Christianity. In other situations, it has resulted in Christianity virtually disappearing. Here are some examples.

In some areas, especially in the past, Christianity seems to have been virtually wiped out of an area. The whole area of North Africa was first a stronghold of Christian faith, with many prominent Christian leaders. Now it is virtually uniformly Muslim. More than 1,000,000 Armenian Christians were forced out of Turkey early in the 20th century during World War II, and Turkey is almost completely Muslim now. The Protestant Huguenots were quite strong in France in the 17th century, and were, in effect, nearly wiped out by the Catholics.

On the other hand, we have seen tremendous growth of Christians in China, to the point that there may be more Christians than communists at this time. About 60 years ago, the communists tried to eliminate the Christian faith. They chased out the missionaries, took over church buildings, and imprisoned or killed Christian leaders. Much of this activity continues. But instead of destroying the church, the communists purified it, answering the prayers of many. Ancestor worship and "rice Christians" were the bane of the Chinese church, hindering growth. The church was considered a western religion of the "foreign devils." Mao came and took the place of a god in the eyes of the people. The little red book of Mao's sayings replaced the Bible as a sacred text. Then Mao died. He left the people, who were virtually worshipping him, without a human god. But the Chinese longed for a true God, the Creator and Redeemer of mankind.

With the elimination of all contact with the west, the church became indigenous. Communism had already undermined ancestor worship. It had become dangerous to be a Christian, and the so-called "rice Christians" who were looking for a handout from the west were also eliminated. The church went underground and became powerful, multiplying from perhaps 1-2,000,000 in 1950 to an estimated 100,000,000 at present. It is ironic that Communism, which sought to eradicate Christianity, has proven one of the most potent sources of her growth.

Another area which has shown explosive growth is the church in southern Sudan (now the new country of South Sudan).

The church underwent severe persecution during World War II with pastors beaten and whipped. The Muslims in the north persecuted the Christian south, often forcing conversions or death, raping women, and enslaving many children. Schools and churches were bombed and destroyed. There has been a longstanding war between the north and south, with an estimated 2,000,000 deaths, mostly of Christians. Nevertheless, schools have been built and churches opened. The number of Christians has greatly increased. The population of the south voted 99% for independence. Many problems have persisted over the last decade, and persecution continues, but the church continues to grow.

Two groups that focus on the needs of the persecuted church are Open Doors, started by Brother Andrew, and Voice of the Martyrs, started by Richard Wurmbrand. Other organizations minister as well. Brother Andrew was better known as "God's Smuggler" and wrote a book by the same name. Richard Wurmbrand was a converted Jew who suffered first under the Nazis, but especially under the communist dictatorship in Romania. He was imprisoned for 14 years, tortured, and kept for three years in a cell 30 feet underground. His wife was also imprisoned and abused. Friends from Norway paid the government $10,000 to release him. In the 1960's, he came to the USA and began his organization to assist those under persecution.

How Can We Assist the Persecuted Church?

These groups have initiated a number of ways to help those under persecution. Some of the effort is to support evangelism. They send Bibles in the appropriate languages and additional materials for Christian growth. Often these must be smuggled into the country. In addition to printed Bibles, with the advent of the digital revolution, much Christian literature can be stored on minidiscs which are much easier to transport and to hide. Cell phones are ubiquitous and make communication much easier. These agencies may provide transportation help, such bicycles, motorbikes, or outboard engines. Voice of the Martyrs also has an airplane which drops materials in Columbia at night into areas held by FARC. Open Doors has smuggled large numbers of Bibles; I believe the largest group was 200 tons of Bibles to China. Some evangelists receive special training to evangelize despite persecution.

Help is also given to the families who have lost husbands. The surviving wives are trained to be able to support themselves. Sometimes they are given grinding machines or sewing machines and are taught to sew. Others are provided with chickens, pigs, oxen, or other animals which they can raise. They may be given financial help until they are able to become self-supporting. Sometimes persons are placed in safe homes away from the persecution - either the individual or members of the family, especially the children. Sometimes help is given to a village. Wells may be drilled or churches and schools that have been destroyed may be rebuilt. The theme verse of Voice of the Martyrs is *Hebrews 13:[3] Remember them that are in bonds, as bound with them; and them which suffer adversity, as being yourself also in the body.* We need to remember that we are one body in Christ. Let us remember to pray for the suffering church and offer material help where we can.

It is important to assist in ways that actually help the persecuted rather than making problems for them. We may focus on the most striking needs such as assistance to those imprisoned or widows, but more strategic assistance may be directed at the basic causes of persecution, which may not be readily apparent.

It is important to define the needs of the persecuted. Sometimes these needs may appear different to different individuals. Some may believe that training resources are most urgent. Others may look at the obvious physical needs. Furthermore, it may not be clear who is best able to meet those particular needs – the church, a NGO, the government, etc., and what is the most effective way to meet the needs without creating more problems for the individuals involved.

We need to be careful about the tactics which we use to assist the persecuted. It is vital that we spend time sorting out the causes of problems and avoid sensationalism or claim results which are not backed by the facts. Publicity which is overheated can backfire and cause problems for those in need. We must be careful that we do not use the persecuted for our own purposes. We must also consider the long term approaches to problems, and realize that there may be multiple solutions to those under persecution so that we do not attack another ministry whose approach may be different from ours. Sometimes quiet diplomacy behind the scenes may accomplish more than a direct confrontation with the persecutors. This is especially true if the direct confrontation may cause the other party to lose face.

At times VIP religious or political leaders have an opportunity to address persecution. However, they may also come with their own agenda, which may at times block their vision of what is happening. Those doing persecution are often quite adept at manipulating propaganda and may deceive those who are visiting to parrot the information which they see, which may be deceptive. We need to be alert to such situations.

Summary of Persecution for Righteousness Sake

In summary, God is a suffering God. He knows our weaknesses and our failings. Jesus learned obedience by the things that He has suffered. We can know that He understands! Thus we can come to God. *Hebrews 4:[15] For we have not a high priest which cannot be touched with feelings of our infirmities: but was in all points tempted like as we are; yet without sin. [16] Let us therefore come boldly unto the throne of grace, that we may obtain mercy, and find grace to help in time of need.*

God has permitted suffering in this world to accomplish his purposes. Persecution is open hostility because we are Christians. All suffering in Christian service, whether sickness or direct persecution, is service both with Christ and for Christ. Satan desires to destroy us through suffering. God plans to use suffering both to purify us and discipline us. Jesus chose suffering. It did not simply come upon Him. It would be foolish to accept a sacrificial lifestyle if there were no life after death. In fact, suffering is a gift of Christ, who chose Himself to suffer. Paul likewise said that if there was no resurrection, it was better not to serve Christ and then die, but just to eat, drink and be merry.

What can be accomplished in suffering? Of course, some suffering occurs simply because we are in a sinful world. And some suffering occurs because of our own sins and foolishness. But suffering for righteousness sake does more than that. Such suffering weans us from self-dependency and magnifies Christ and His grace. Jesus learned obedience from the suffering. But He never sinned, so His suffering was not from sin. Suffering for righteousness shows the lie of Satan, who has built his kingdom of darkness on power and authority, and not on love and compassion.

God wants us to have an impact. He wants us to be passionate for Him. Paul wanted to know that one thing — to glorify God through Christ. We must boast in the cross of Christ, where everything good was obtained for sinners. Further, we only boast in the cross when we are on the cross. The old self dies, and the new self lives by the faith of God in Christ Jesus. We boast in the cross when we bear the cross. Then Christ is all in life or in death. He indeed will be honored. Death makes visible where our values and our treasure truly are. And when we trust Christ, we trust Him to give us that one thing which we need most, which is Himself! Paul wanted to magnify Christ in life or death. When we die daily we live for Christ daily. We are perfected through trials and pain, and thus we, like the disciples, experience joy as we grow in our faith.

God gives blessings with His grace. Persons will receive Christ. Often God uses the forgiveness of the one being persecuted to draw the very persecutor to Himself. We see this in the Bible with Stephen and Paul, and then later Paul and the Philippian jailor. There are a number of stories where the persecutors themselves become believers and join those they have persecuted. Through our proper response to persecution, we demonstrate the grace of God, which is sufficient in all situations. God can use the very same persecutions which Satan uses to attack the believers to draw those under Satan's power to Himself.

The goal in life is to make others rejoice in God forever as they receive Jesus Christ as their Savior. To draw others to Christ, we must forgive. Then our conscience is free from bitterness allowing us to love not only God but also the individual. We must show in our lives the fact that God has already forgiven us. The goal is to give others eternal joy, which requires the grace of God. We can accomplish these purposes as we suffer for righteousness in the power and grace of God.

What can suffering do in our own personal lives? Suffering shows our motives and demonstrates our priorities. Suffering draws us close to Christ. And God gives us further blessings in the future. We can anticipate glory in heaven. *2 Corinthians 4:[16] For which cause we faint not; but though our outward man perish, yet the inward man is renewed day by day. [17] For our light affliction, which is but for a moment, worketh for us a far more exceeding and eternal weight of glory; [18] While we look not at the things which are seen, but at the things which are not seen: for the things which are seen are temporal; but the things which are not seen are eternal.*

Paul, who certainly earned the right to write these words, may have suffered more than any other missionary in the New Testament. But he was victorious. *Romans 8:[16] The spirit itself beareth witness with our spirit, that we are the children of God: [17] And if children, then heirs; heirs of God, and joint-heirs with Christ; if so be that we suffer with him, that we may be also glorified together. [18] For I reckon that the sufferings of the present time are not worthy to be compared with the glory which shall be revealed in us.* Thus: no suffering, no glory. But as we suffer for Christ, there is comfort and future glory for both ourselves and others.

This demonstrates the power of God and the power Holy Spirit. Through persecution, we learn that we cannot build our lives successfully for God when we build upon ourselves. But if we suffer with Him, we will reign with Him. Thereby we clearly demonstrate the worth of Jesus Christ, who is worth more than family, goods, position, and life itself.

The Urgent versus the Strategic:

Long term strategy may ultimately yield greater results than focusing simply on the urgent. The urgent is important, but if we allow this to distract us from proper long-term strategy, this is a great detriment to us. Let me give a couple medical examples.

When I went to Liberia, West Africa, I was able to study a plan for medical care for the country which had been developed a few years before I arrived there, which included a 40-bed hospital for smallpox. Smallpox had been a problem, but with proper vaccinations, it was basically eliminated and I never saw a case. A similar situation in the USA occurred with tuberculosis and with polio. Before the development of polio vaccine, there were hospitals filled with ventilators to keep polio patients alive. Likewise, when I was in medical school, effective medication for tuberculosis was developed. The sanitaria which were filled with patients emptied out and were used for other sicknesses.

At the present time we in the United States are reaping the rewards of ignoring secular education for more than 50 years. Socialism and Marxism have been taught in the public schools for decades, and most secular universities teach policies which are not Biblical. The same thing may be true in places where the persecution is more open, although we who are teaching have been experiencing some persecution such as failure to secure a position or tenure, termination of teaching positions, and distain of our positions and beliefs. The country is struggling with abortion, transgender policies, same-sex marriages, etc. As long as the educational system and media remain unchallenged and unchanged, we can anticipate the same problems. Thus we need to be alert to underlying causes and correct them while not ignoring acute needs. We must attack lies with truth.

How Can We Help the Persecuted Church without Hurting Them?

We have seen that we indeed have a responsibility to our persecuted brothers and sisters in Christ. We have also seen that the causes of persecution are often multiple and complex. Sometimes our best efforts result in more harm than good. What can we do to help without hurting? Here are a number of observations, again from Faith that Endures.

1. Prayer: The uniform answer of the persecuted is for prayer. They recognize the need of prayer especially since often they have only recourse to prayer. One Chinese leader who was confined to prison for over 20 years gave three reasons for requesting prayer:
   a. Prayer blesses the one praying. We who have many options open to us do not spend the time to really experience God's blessing
   b. Prayer gives a greater burden for those who are undergoing persecution. Those who are praying are more likely to help in other ways as the Lord leads
   c. God has bound Himself to answer when we pray to Him in trust.
2. Publicity: It is usually OK to speak on behalf of the persecuted church, but not always for persecuted individuals. Most of the time, the Chinese leaders did not want publicity for 2 reasons. First, they said that to be jailed is to be rewarded, and they did not want to lose their reward. Second, with so much publicity, they

would be shadowed forever by the secret police and lose their future ministry instead of being able to resume it after release. However, there were four suggestions made for individuals who are persecuted.

    a. The individual or their family must give permission
    b. Talk with the local church leadership
    c. Use it as a last resort. It may hinder the ministry of the individual
    d. The publicity must not disclose any information gift to the authorities

It may be difficult to get this accepted. Some individuals will not acknowledge that religion would result in persecution. The documents are also often scanty because of the nature of persecution. Sometimes political correctness will make it difficult for some to accept the truth of the persecution. And sometimes those leaders who could support the persecuted are too afraid of consequences to do so.

3. Personal contacts: Informally persons may be able to influence release of the persecuted. Often, they will write letters, one encouraging the persecuted, and one to the persecutor.

4. Legal intervention: Many places that persecute could care less about whether persecution is legal or not. But charging them with overreaching their legal rights may influence them because they do not want the stigma associated with the persecution. Others may not be aware of their rights which are being violated and have courage to stand up to the persecutors. It takes wisdom to know which approach is the best at the time. The apostle Paul was frequently thrown into jail, often on false charges. On some occasions he failed to object; on other occasions he insisted on his rights as a Roman citizen. He did so at Philippi when he was unjustly jailed without due process and the rulers wanted to send him

away quietly without acknowledging their fault, once when he was about to be scourged without a proper trial, and once when he appealed to Caesar to avoid almost certain death at the hands of the Jews.

5. Illegal intervention: When commanded not to preach Jesus and the resurrection from the dead, Peter flatly refused to obey the Sanhedrin. He stated that they must obey God rather than man. This may, of course, result in various forms of punishment. But it also may result in changing an unjust law and permitting the restricted behavior in the future.

6. Political pressure at the individual or governmental level: The ability to change the basic nature of the persecutor is quite limited through the government, but it may be helpful at times. Sometimes the greatest help is making the government aware that persecution is really occurring, and that support should be offered to those being persecuted.

7. Positive engagement: Christians can continue to build up the society in which the persecution is occurring. This may involve improving education, providing schools and instructors, or improving health, providing hospitals and medical personnel, or helping in the agricultural sector or business, or building orphanages. You hope to build mutual trust.

What Lessons Can We Learn from the Persecuted Church?

We often ask what we should be doing for the persecuted church. One of those things is accepting the lessons which they can provide for us. We are both parts of the body of Christ. We have a responsibility to minister to the suffering parts of the body. But we also have a responsibility to allow them to minister to us.

1. We must learn to slow down and cultivate a relationship

with God. One of the benefits of being thrown in jail was to be forced to slow down.

    a. Richard Wurmbrand was jailed for 14 years. For three years, he was in solitary confinement thirty feet below the ground. His guards would wear slippers so that he would not hear them approach. His food was simply shoved through a slot to him. The human waste was removed. Many persons became insane. Instead, he developed a relationship with God. He preached many sermons to the walls. But his relationship with God deepened.

    b. Wang Mingdao spent over 20 years confined to prison when he was at the peak of his powers as an evangelist. He could no longer preach, write, study the Bible and witness. But he drew close to God during that time.

    c. When the apostle Paul was confined to prison for years, again at the peak of his intellectual powers, he also had to slow down his tremendous pace. In ten years, he had basically impacted four Roman provinces for God, but now he could not travel. However, during that time he produced his prison epistles, perhaps the greatest depths of insight and an inconceivable present to the church.

2. It may be difficult for the persecuted individuals to make any sense of their lives. They are no longer in control. But the persecuted will learn that God is in control, and that we can trust Him. It is not our responsibility to figure out why certain things in our lives occur. As God said in *Isaiah 55:8-9 For my thoughts are not your thoughts, neither are your ways my ways, saith the Lord. For as the heavens are higher than the earth, so are my ways higher than your ways, and my thoughts than your thoughts....11. So shall my word be that goeth forth out of my mouth; it shall not return unto me void, but it shall*

accomplish that which I please, and it shall prosper in the thing whereto I sent it.

It is important to recognize that God is still ultimately in control of His world. He is the Creator of the World and its Redeemer. He will use us in ways which we never suspected, and He will protect us also from both outside situations and from ourselves. Although I would not consider myself very persecuted, I can attest that several times I was disappointed that plans which I had made did not come to fruition only later to see the great wisdom in God's saying "No." Those who are persecuted have little choice – they must accept many things which we would normally not desire. But God shows Himself faithful to them in ways which we would not expect.

3. God builds His kingdom not with our abilities as much as our sacrifices. That is why consumerism is so antithetical to our spiritual growth in the Lord. In times of persecution, often we can contribute little, but we are emptied of self. Then the Lord promises to never leave us nor forsake us and comes to fill us with Himself. The emptier we are, the more He can fill us. *Mark 8:34-35 And when he had called the people unto him with his disciples also, he said unto them, Whosoever will come after me, let him deny himself, and take up his creoss, and follow me. For whosoever will save his life shall lose it; but whosoever shall lose his life for my sake and the gospel's, the same shall save it.*

We have many idols in the world. During the first three centuries after Christ, the idol was Caesar. In China during the cultural revolution, Mao presented himself as a man-made "God" and thus an idol. We in the west also have many idols, all clamoring for our worship. Often the idols are part of materialism: a bigger and better house or car, or bank account. Or perhaps it is a bigger name to revel in. Anything which urges us to place it first and God second is an idol. When we fail to worship the idols of the world, the world strikes back, and often we suffer persecution.

The persecution in other lands is often physical, sometimes even resulting in death. In the West, we are more likely to have psychological persecution, with discouragement, depression, and discrimination. We too are in war against the world system, our old fleshly nature, and Satan himself. We too can expect persecution when we live godly in Christ Jesus, as Paul states in *2 Timothy 3:12 Yea, and all that will live godly in Christ Jesus shall suffer persecution.*

We are indeed in a battle. Our hearts are part of the battle. They may be reluctant to war against the enemy. The world battles against us and blinds us with the allure of the things of this world. Furthermore, we face the lies of the devil who may tell us we are no good, or, on the other hand, we are so good that we do not need to get saved. We are in a spiritual battle, and will need to use weapons of the Spirit to win.

How Big is My God?

We in the West have relatively few emergencies. Those in persecuted countries may have weekly emergencies. When the Jewish nation of slaves left Egypt and crossed the wilderness to Canaan, they faced formidable foes – both human opponents and physical challenges. God was able to deliver them in amazing supernatural ways. Further, God sustained them through trials over a 40-year period.

God uses our weaknesses to display His grace and creative power. He is able to use us despite our weakness, or perhaps because of our weakness. This is frequently displayed by our endurance despite prolonged persecution and brings great glory to God. The persecuted Christian may have no understanding of what God is doing. He leaves his future in the hands of God, content with knowing that God is a God of love who wants the very best for His children. As we humbly submit to His hands to mold us as He wishes, He is able to use us and to obtain great glory doing so.

A Summary of Suffering, Martyrdom, and Rewards in Heaven

I would like to conclude with a brief summary of my understanding of Josef Ton's book, *Suffering, Martyrdom, and Rewards in Heaven*, written in 1997.[30] It is significant that when Ton wrote this book, he was facing a decision: whether or not to return to Romania to work. He knew that he would face persecution from the communist dictatorship and possible martyrdom himself. At the conclusion of the book, he found the solution to the questions he had been asking. He was prepared to return and face martyrdom if that was God's will for his life.

Ton begins with the plan of God to give man dominion over all His works for eternity. His plan was temporarily thwarted by the fall of man, but mankind was restored to relationship with God through the redemption of Jesus Christ. God's plan was to bring many believers to maturity. They would resemble His Son, and they would have charge of His possessions. God is using the trials and troubles of this fallen world to conform us to the image of His Son, and to develop the character we need to rule with Him. The final reward of ruling with Him is called with a variety of names such as: our inheritance, reigning with Christ, being glorified with Christ, or gaining treasures or rewards in heaven. This dominion is indicated in man's creation in Genesis 1:26-28, and also in Psalm 8, Hebrews 2:5-13, and in Romans 8.

Suffering and persecution are two of the most effective tools the Lord uses to form us like Christ. God wants us to develop a blameless character, which will be demonstrated by examining our works at the judgment seat of Christ. The character we develop here will continue into eternity, and the judge will determine our worthiness of rewards based on our character and works. The rewards are in terms of responsibility and authority. However, we do not earn or merit these ourselves. God has given each believer the Holy Spirit and His divine nature, but man must cooperate to develop what God intends. God and man work hand in hand, but ultimately the source of all blessing is God, and it comes to us through His grace.

God calls His people to total allegiance to Himself. He knows that the world will react with violence against the witness of His children. His children must meet this hatred with love, and this violence with submission to the will of God. God must be above family, position, and possessions. The disciple is a slave of Christ, totally at His disposal. The goal of the witness is not to die, but to witness to the truth. If God calls the individual to martyrdom, he must be willing. Not all are called to martyrdom, but the true disciple will undergo suffering and live sacrificially for the gospel. Some will be called to a quick death, some to a slow lingering death, and others will not be called to martyrdom. Ton believes that the scriptures indicate that there may well be a fixed number of martyrs.

God's Plan is to Accomplish Three Things Through Martyrdom:

First, God's truth triumphs. The entire world lies in darkness. The eyes of the unbeliever are blinded by the god of this world. Just as someone who lives in darkness will react against a sudden light, the world reacts against the believer. Jesus warned His disciples in John 3:19-20 that the world would reject the light because their deeds were darkness. However, with the death of the martyr, the eyes of the lost are opened to the truth and beauty of God's word. Often it takes the death of the missionary before the lost in a new area come to Christ.

Secondly, Satan is defeated. Satan keeps mankind in slavery through the fear of death. Christ nailed the punishment of our sins on the cross (Colossians 2:14-15), paying the death penalty in our place. He released us from the fear of death as well at the cross (Hebrews 2:14-15). When the martyr meets his death without fear, Satan's hold is broken. As the light of the gospel shines, the nations which were in darkness turn to the light. We see further demonstrations of this truth in the life of Job, who was a testimony not only on earth, but especially to the angels in heaven. Paul refers to the same concept for the apostles as well. (1 Cor. 4:9)

Thirdly, martyrdom brings glory to God. Christ demonstrated to the world God's unconditional love even in the most painful and shameful type of public execution, the death by crucifixion. Likewise, the disciple who bears suffering for righteousness also brings glory to God. God is shown as worth more than family, friends, position, health, or life itself. John mentions the type of death by which Peter will glorify God (John 21:19). He is speaking of Peter's death as a martyr.

So far, I do not think that many would argue with Ton's analysis. But he comes now to a very important question. It appears very clear that our life on earth will make a difference for our eternal life with Christ. The Bible speaks many times concerning rewards. Jesus mentions it a number of times both directly and in parables. Paul mentions it on several occasions as well. Are these rewards that we earn, or are they by grace? What is the nature of the rewards, and how are they obtained?

First, Ton is very clear that he rejects any concept that we actually merit or earn rewards. Rewards are the gift of God, and not a payment for service rendered to God. Furthermore, as we receive these by grace, this grace is not our personal possession. He totally rejects the Catholic concept of grace being obtained by the saints to be used through the church for others who are in spiritual need.

God wants to see three basic character traits exhibited in our lives. The first is obedience to God. Although God gives His children free will, He wants to see them freely choose what God Himself wants as the best choice in their lives. Thus they fully obey Him and submit to Him. Secondly, they have an agape-love for each other shown by willing self-sacrifice and service for others. Thirdly, they exhibit wisdom, applying God's commandments to all situations.

Suffering is a key method for God to develop these three

traits in His children. Jesus Christ was made perfect through suffering (Hebrews 2:10) and learned obedience through the things which He suffered. (Heb. 5:8) God treats us like sons as He disciplines us to develop within us the character He desires. (Heb. 12:5-11) Both Paul (Romans 5:1-5) and James (James 1:2-12) teach that God uses trials to mold us and produce those characteristics in our lives.

God's chosen disciples are to seek to be conformed to Christ's image. They are not to seek suffering in itself. God will choose what type of suffering - arrests, persecution, torture and even martyrdom may be required to inscribe the proper character in the life of the disciple. Thus the suffering does more than provide an opportunity to witness, but actually changes the character of the individual. In the early centuries after Christ, they called it the "perfecting" of the martyr.

An additional concept is that of testing the disciple. Jesus tells four times of a king leaving his subjects alone with responsibilities he has entrusted to them. After a long time, he returns to reward the slave according to his faithfulness to the task. (Mt. 24:45-51; 25:14-30; Lk. 12:35-48, & 19:11-27.) He then concludes with the parable of the unfaithful steward found in Luke 16:1-13. He makes three important points. (1) He who is faithful in small things will be faithful in larger things, but he who is unfaithful in small things is unfaithful in large things. (2) Things of the earth are not the true riches. They are temporary - but they are useful to test our faithfulness. (3) What we have on earth is not our own. We are "slaves" or stewards. God has a great reward in eternity for us, but will only entrust it to those who are worthy. This does not mean that they earn the reward, but that they show the kind of responsibility that is able to receive the reward.

It is at the judgment seat of Christ that we will learn whether we have been "approved" or "disapproved." Paul was very concerned that he not be disapproved (1 Cor. 9:24-27). But since God provides His children with all they need, they do not earn the reward. The reward is from the generosity of God through the grace He extends to His children.

Then Ton gives a warning to the relatively affluent west. He points out that the affluence itself is a test to see if the believer will spend virtually all on himself or on others as well. The temptation is to keep the wealth, which can have an increasing hold on the believer. Our blessings and riches on earth can be the very thing that results in our poverty in heaven.

Although riches can be a test, the test of suffering and martyrdom is an even more severe and higher test. Jesus Christ gave up the riches in heaven, the most riches of all, for the suffering and shame of the cross. Therefore His name is above all names. (Phil. 2:5-11) Furthermore, suffering and martyrdom play an important role as a witness to God's love for mankind, as well as a method of transforming man into the image of His Son. When we recognize this fact, our suffering no longer is senseless, but is a part of God's program to make us like Jesus.

Addendum

Some Thoughts From Paul Marshall: Their Blood Cries Out:[31]

Marshall notes again that there is an enormous amount of persecution for religious reasons today, with the Christians taking the main brunt of the persecution, but other religions receiving some as well. However, most persons are either unaware of the persecution, or rather indifferent to it. In the past, Christian persecution of other Christians was quite common, especially the Roman Catholic Church persecuting Protestants and Baptists, but this has also occurred many times with the Orthodox church as well. Both groups have also persecuted other religions, especially Jews.

However, the two primarily groups doing persecution at the present time are the Muslims and the Communists. Radical Hindus and Buddhists are also involved in persecution. What is

161

striking is that the most persecution occurs in countries that are the most totalitarian. This is true for the Muslims, where often there is a "strong man." This is also true for the communists, who want basically a totalitarian state although they speak of the eventual rise of the common man. This is also true of the structure of both the Roman Catholic Church and the Orthodox Church. True believers are usually contributors to society, and often at the forefront of human rights and development of democracy. Furthermore, they believe in the ultimate authority of a higher power rather than the immediate authority figure of the country or religion - and this is difficult for a totalitarian group to tolerate. Thus they react, often violently, against anyone who dares to oppose their unilateral power.

Why is There Minimal Response from the United States?

There are a number of different reasons for the lack of response from such countries as the USA. First, the media, which must provide the information, is liberal, and often ignorant of Christian belief or prejudiced against it. Many of the mainline churches associated with the National Council of Churches or the World Council of Churches are also liberal. They feel no urgency to present the gospel to others, and may feel that the Christians called down the persecution upon themselves. This is particularly true in the postmodern mentality of the USA, with its emphasis on political correctness and the absence of absolutes. America is also mostly self-focused, and can hardly conceive of others willing to die for their beliefs. Persecution makes them uncomfortable. They sense no responsibility toward believers in other nations.

The book by Marshall documents case after case of persecution throughout the world. Some of the information in the book is outlined above, and for further details, I would recommend reading the book as well. It is clear and well-written, although the challenge does not make for "comfortable reading." We need to be praying for those under persecution and reaching out to them as well.

Again, we are reminded of Jesus' statement in *Matthew 25:[31] When the Son of man shall come in his glory, and all the holy angels with him, then shall he sit upon the throne of his glory:[32] And before him shall be gathered all nations: and he shall separate them one from another, as a shepherd divideth his sheep from the goats:[33] And he shall set the sheep on his right hand, but the goats on the left.[34] Then shall the King say unto them on his right hand, Come, ye blessed of my Father, inherit the kingdom prepared for you from the foundation of the world:[35] For I was an hungred, and ye gave me meat: I was thirsty, and ye gave me drink: I was a stranger, and ye took me in:[36] Naked, and ye clothed me: I was sick, and ye visited me: I was in prison, and ye came unto me.[37] Then shall the righteous answer him, saying, Lord, when saw we thee an hungred, and fed thee? or thirsty, and gave thee drink?[38] When saw we thee a stranger, and took thee in? or naked, and clothed thee?[39] Or when saw we thee sick, or in prison, and came unto thee?[40] And the King shall answer and say unto them, Verily I say unto you, Inasmuch as ye have done it unto one of the least of these my brethren, ye have done it unto me.[41] Then shall he say also unto them on the left hand, Depart from me, ye cursed, into everlasting fire, prepared for the devil and his angels:[42] For I was an hungred, and ye gave me no meat: I was thirsty, and ye gave me no drink:[43] I was a stranger, and ye took me not in: naked, and ye clothed me not: sick, and in prison, and ye visited me not.[44] Then shall they also answer him, saying, Lord, when saw we thee an hungred, or athirst, or a stranger, or naked, or sick, or in prison, and did not minister unto thee?[45] Then shall he answer them, saying, Verily I say unto you, Inasmuch as ye did it not to one of the least of these, ye did it not to me.[46] And these shall go away into everlasting punishment: but the righteous into life eternal.*

Where do we fit in this challenge of Jesus?

Questions For Persecution

1. Which of the following is true:
   a. The period of greatest persecution with martyrs was in the fourth century
   b. The majority of those persecuted are Muslims
   c. Persecution actually may help spread the church
   d. All of the above are true
   e. a & b are true, but c is false
   f. a & c are true, but b is false
   g. b & c are true, but a is false
2. The New Testament was written by persecuted believers, and largely for persecuted believers.
   a. True
   b. False
3. It would be a great surprise if Christians are persecuted for doing right.
   a. True
   b. False
4. The message of the church is cross-centered, and we need cross-centered messengers.
   a. True
   b. False
5. What facts about creation are important to understanding persecution?
   a. Man is created in the image of God
   b. Man has intrinsic worth and respect
   c. God's character is the foundation of the basis of law
   d. He expects us to act toward others as He acts toward us
   e. All of the above are true
   f. All of the above except b are true
   g. All the above except d are true

6.   What are the minimal rights that God expects us to provide for vulnerable persons?
      a.   The right to die, including suicide
      b.   The right of property
      c.   The necessities of life
      d.   The right to live unharmed
      e.   All of the above are true
      f.   All of the above except a are true
      g.   All of the above except b are true
7.   God shows concern about abuse to certain vulnerable groups, including the following:
      a.   Strangers
      b.   Orphans
      c.   Widows
      d.   Terrorists
      e.   All of the above
      f.   All the above except a
      g.   All the above except d
8.   God wants us protected against:
      a.   Abortion
      b.   Physical abuse
      c.   Being taken hostage
      d.   All of the above
      e.   a & b are true, but c is false
      f.   a & c are true, but b is false
      g.   b & c are true, but a is false
9.   Which groups recognize that man is created in the image of God?
      a.   Judaism
      b.   Christianity
      c.   Islam
      d.   Communism
      e.   All of the above
      f.   a & b are true, but c & d are false
      g.   c & d are true, but a & b are false
10.   The fact that God is a trinity shows the importance of

relationships in context with individual rights.
a. True
b. False

11. God created us with the ability to choose the right, but also to choose the wrong.
a. True
b. False

12. What is true about rights?
a. Public rights come from God, and need to be defended
b. Private rights sometimes can be voluntarily yielded for the sake of Christ
c. The advancement of God's kingdom should be our first consideration
d. All of the above are correct
e. a & b are true, but c is false
f. a & c are true, but b is false
g. b & c are true, but a is false

13. Restoration of man to God involves suffering of the deliverer.
a. True
b. False

14. In the fall, both man and woman were involved in suffering.
a. True
b. False

15. What is true about God's redeeming love?
a. God created man with free choice, knowing that man would fall
b. True love requires freedom of choice
c. Redemption involves pain and suffering
d. All of the above
e. a & b are true, but c is false
f. a & c are true, but b is false
g. b & c are true, but a is false

16. The first religious persecution was:

      a.   Cain and Abel
      b.   The first murder
      c.   In the context of worship
      d.   In the context of family
      e.   All of the above
      f.   All of the above are true except c
      g.   a & b are true, but c & d are false

17.   After the time of Noah, God:
      a.   Said that the death penalty is abolished
      b.   Made mankind responsible to uphold God's justice
      c.   Placed the authority for the death penalty in the hands of civil authorities
      d.   All of the above
      e.   a & b are true, but c is false
      f.   a & c are true, but b is false
      g.   b & c are true, but a is false

18.   What is true about persecution?
      a.   Only strong believers will be persecuted
      b.   All claiming to follow God may be challenged to take a stand
      c.   Those who are stronger are more likely to be persecuted
      d.   All of the above
      e.   a & b are true, but c is false
      f.   a & c are true, but b is false
      g.   b & c are true, but a is false

19.   Some lessons of the Penteteuch:
      a.   Suffering and trials are part of life
      b.   True faith will have trials and suffering
      c.   True greatness may come as one chooses to suffer for God's plan to be fulfilled
      d.   All of the above are true
      e.   a & b are true, but c is false
      f.   a & c are true, but b is false
      g.   b & c are true, but a is false

20. What are some lessons from the Pentateuch?
  a. Suffering can become a blessing if we glorify God with it
  b. Suffering is sometimes a part of God's plan to bring His people back to Himself
  c. Suffering may be the result of continuing in sin
  d. Suffering and sin are permanent
  e. All of the above are true
  f. a & b are true, but c & d are false
  g. All the above except d are true
21. Sometimes God's blessings become curses if we fail to glorify God in the blessing.
  a. True
  b. False
22. Lessons from Job about suffering:
  a. All suffering is caused by our sin
  b. As soon as we stop sinning, our suffering will stop
  c. Suffering people always need our advice, not just our presence
  d. Job's friends are an excellent example of how to help a sufferer
  e. All of the above are true
  f. b & c are true, but a & d are false
  g. All the above are false
23. Lessons from Job concerning suffering:
  a. God will always show us why we are suffering
  b. The most important lesson to learn is to trust the Lord
  c. God called on Job's friends to repent, although they had not suffered
  d. Job, who spoke rightly about God, did suffer
  e. All of the above are true
  f. All but a are true
  g. a & b are true, but c & d are false
24. Lessons from Isaiah on suffering:

a. Suffering may occur as punishment for sin
b. Suffering may help establish your relationship with God
c. Suffering may be for training and education
d. God works through the suffering servant who suffers for others' sins
e. All of the above are true
f. a & b are true, but c & d are false
g. c & d are true, but a & b are false

25. Those who follow the suffering servant are likely to suffer and sacrifice, but also to manifest God's power.
a. True
b. False

26. Jeremiah's situation with suffering:
a. He was amazed that the people would reject his message
b. He knew that his message was from God
c. He had a great love for his people despite their persecution of him
d. All the above are true
e. a & b are true, but c is false
f. a & c are true, but b is false
g. b & c are true, but a is false

27. Daniel teaches us:
a. God is sovereign in history, and He will ultimately prevail
b. God never shares His authority with man
c. If necessary, we must be willing to be faithful to death
d. All of the above are true
e. a & b are true, but c is false
f. a & c are true, but b is false
g. b & c are true, but a is false

28. What kind of people will rule with God, according to Daniel?
a. Those who obey God and His laws despite

personal cost
b.   Those who remain true to God despite persecution
c.   Those who see God's reign in everything
d.   Those who declare the power and glory of God to those around them
e.   All of the above are true
f.   c & d are true, but a & b are false
g.   a & b are true, but c & d are false

29.   What is true about God and suffering?
a.   God is far above His creation, and He never suffers
b.   The cross is central in revealing the nature of God
c.   God shares our pain
d.   All of the above are true
e.   a & b are true, but c is false
f.   a & c are true, but b is false
g.   b & c are true, but a is false

30.   God is self-giving and works through persuasion and sacrifice rather than power and force.
a.   True
b.   False

31.   We present the gospel incorrectly when:
a.   We seek our own glory rather than the glory of God
b.   We use physical force or psychological pressure
c.   We misrepresent God or Jesus Christ
d.   All of the above show incorrect ways to present the gospel
e.   None of the above are incorrect, because the end justifies the means
f.   b & c are true, but a is false
g.   a & c are true, but b is false

32.   In the Sermon on the Mount, what does Jesus show us about suffering?
a.   Those who suffer are in the line of the prophets
b.   We must never rejoice

     c.   We must love those who persecute us

     d.   We are actually in service to our persecutors

     e.   All of the above are true

     f.   All of the above except b are true

     g.   c & d are true, but a & b are false

33.   We learn the following principles in the beatitudes:

     a.   We are the possessors of the kingdom of heaven if we suffer for righteousness sake

     b.   Suffering is never expected of true messengers of God; God blesses all His messengers, and suffering is a sign that we are outside His will

     c.   Persecution never comes to a true messenger of God; others will not try to stop the message or the messenger

     d.   All of the above are true

     e.   a & b are true, but c is false

     f.   a & c are true, but b is false

     g.   b & c are true, but a is false

34.   Jesus uses the illustration of sending us like sheep in the midst of wolves.

     a.   This shows that survival is not the ultimate issue

     b.   Jesus Himself was portrayed in Isaiah 53 as a lamb brought to the slaughter

     c.   What is important is our message given through word and deed

     d.   Mission and persecution go together

     e.   All of the above are true

     f.   a, b & c are true, but d is false

     g.   All of the above except a are true

35.   What are real dangers in persecution?

     a.   Fear and compromising the truth

     b.   Deliberately provoking authorities to attract persecution

     c.   Suffering for our faith

     d.   All of the above

     e.   a & b are true, but c is false

f.   a & c are true, but b is false

g.   b & c are true, but a is false

36.   Truth about persecution:

    a.   Persecution can separate the believer from God

    b.   Persecution can expose a faith that is just profession, but not true belief

    c.   Persecution not only brings suffering, but also permanent destruction of the person persecuted

    d.   All of the above are true

    e.   a & b are true, but c is false

    f.   a & c are true, but b is false

    g.   b & c are true, but a is false

37.   What is true about persecution?

    a.   Flight from persecution is always wrong

    b.   It is wrong to flee persecution just to avoid suffering

    c.   Jesus never hid from persecution

    d.   Paul never hid from persecution

    e.   All of the above are true

    f.   b & d are true, but a & c are false

    g.   a & c are true, but b & d are false

38.   What are possible biblical responses to persecution?

    a.   Flight

    b.   Fight for rights

    c.   Fortitude - standing until death

    d.   All of the above

    e.   a & b are true, but c is false

    f.   a & c are true, but b is false

    g.   b & c are true, but a is false

39.   Jesus said that we must not fear man, but God. Which of the following is/are true?

    a.   Man can harm the body, but not the soul

    b.   God will bring the body back to life, so man's persecution is limited at best

    c.   The real threat is not to be all that God wants us to be

       d.   All of the above are true

       e.   a & b are true, but c is false

       f.   a & c are true, but b is false

       g.   b & c are true, but a is false

40.   Dangers for the believer in persecution:

       a.   Acknowledging Christ

       b.   Loving family more than Christ

       c.   Loving our life more than Christ

       d.   Refusing to receive those who are wanted by authorities because of their witness for Christ

       e.   All of the above are true

       f.   All the above except a are true

       g.   All of the above are true except b

41.   What does Jesus teach us about persecution in Mt. 16:21-28?

       a.   There are great rewards for faithfulness in persecution

       b.   Training in this life is useful for tasks in eternity

       c.   We receive rewards when we receive His grace and suffer and serve for His sake

       d.   We receive rewards when we renounce the world (asceticism) just to get rewards

       e.   All of the above are true

       f.   All the above are true except b

       g.   All the above are true except d

42.   Which is true?

       a.   We should focus on Christ and His purposes

       b.   The true disciple knows the sacrifice he has made, and anticipates the rewards for his hard work

       c.   Both are true

       d.   Neither is true

43.   Which is true?

       a.   The cross is the path to glory for Christ

       b.   The cross is the path to glory for the believer

       c.   Both are true

       d.   Neither is true

44. We can expect persecution because Jesus was hated, and those who hate Jesus will also hate His followers.
    a. True
    b. False

45. Persecution always works in the lives of all believers to make them witness for Christ, and for them to become stronger believers.
    a. True
    b. False

46. (Jn. 12:32) Jesus drew *all* men to Himself when:
    a. He did signs and wonders
    b. He was lifted up
    c. Both
    d. Neither

47. For a corn of wheat to bring forth much fruit, first it must die.
    a. True
    b. False

48. In the book of Acts, we see the Holy Spirit in action:
    a. He gives them power and authority when they speak
    b. He is their comforter in persecution
    c. He initiates through the believer; thus the believer is not merely passive.
    d. He uses persecution to provide more opportunities to witness
    e. All of the above are true
    f. a & b are true, but c & d are false
    g. c & d are true, but a & b are false

49. Reasons for persecution include:
    a. Religious - threatening the existing system
    b. Political - primary loyalty to the nation, not to Christ
    c. Social - upset social and family norms
    d. Economic - certain businesses become difficult
    e. Emotional - jealousy, especially by religious leaders

f.   All of the above are true

g.   All of the above except b are true

50.   The apostles were willing to die because:

a.   They knew that God was sovereign

b.   They saw suffering for Christ as a privilege

c.   They saw the glory of martyrdom

d.   All of the above are true

e.   a & b are true, but c is false

f.   a & c are true, but b is false

g.   b & c are true, but a is false

51.   What is true?

a.   The persecutors of God's people stand in the line of God's prophets

b.   The religious leaders often persecuted God's agents

c.   Persecution is never in the plan of God

d.   All of the above are true

e.   a & b are true, but c is false

f.   a & c are true, but b is false

g.   b & c are true, but a is false

52.   The true witness?

a.   Depends on the Holy Spirit, and not his own wisdom

b.   Preaches the cross rather than human wisdom

c.   Ministers in weakness rather than his own strength

d.   Demonstrates a Christ-like character

e.   All of the above

f.   All of the above except a are true

g.   All of the above are true except c

53.   What is the relationship between suffering and inheritance?

a.   We experience no suffering, bur great inheritance shared with Christ

b.   We experience no suffering, but great glory shared with Christ

      c.   Persecution prepares us for the responsibilities which we will inherit

      d.   Our method of ministry must align with Christ's method, which is the cross

      e.   All of the above are true

      f.   a & b are true, but c & d are false

      g.   c & d are true, but a & b are false

54.   The key issue is which of the following:

      a.   Why we suffer

      b.   If we suffer

      c.   How we suffer

55.   What is the relationship between persecution and the cross

      a.   Many avoid the cross to avoid persecution

      b.   The cross not only crucifies the world to me, but me to the world

      c.   Both are true

      d.   Neither is true

56.   The mission of the messenger of Christ is:

      a.   Self-serving rather than incarnational

      b.   Self-preserving rather than the cross

      c.   Weakness and dependency rather than stability and strength

      d.   All of the above are true

      e.   a & b are true, but c is false

      f.   a & c are true, but b is false

      g.   b & c are true, but a is false

57.   What is true?

      a.   To abandon the cross is to abandon Christ

      b.   The natural man will accept the message of the cross when he sees it

      c.   We should work in our own weakness and foolishness depending on His strength

      d.   All of the above are true

      e.   a & b are true, but c is false

      f.   a & c are true, but b is false

g.   b & c are true, but a is false

58.   For effective communication of the gospel, the Holy Spirit must demonstrate Himself in

a.   The message

b.   The messenger

c.   Both are true

d.   Neither is true

59.   Both the believer and unbeliever will view the sufferings of the apostle Paul in the same manner.

a.   True

b.   False

60.   The church can be true to her calling and also "seeker sensitive" at the same time.

a.   True

b.   False

61.   Who or what is glorious concerning the gospel?

a.   The message

b.   The messenger

c.   Both

d.   Neither

62.   Suffering:

a.   Earns our right to heavenly reward through our good works

b.   For righteousness may well put us in positions of authority in the future

c.   For righteousness through the cross is the same method of Christ

d.   All of the above are true

e.   a & b are true, but c is false

f.   a & c are true, but b is false

g.   b & c are true, but a is false

63.   Results of Paul's imprisonment included:

a.   The non-Christians knew why Paul was in prison

b.   The Christians took heart when they saw Paul's victorious attitude

c.   Paul showed that his method of victory was his

priority: that Christ would be preached and glorified
d. All of the above are true
e. a & b are true, but c is false
f. b & c are true, but a is false
g. a & c are true, but b is false

64. Joy is dependent upon our
a. Priorities
b. Circumstances

65. The resurrection of the dead that Paul mentions in 3:10 is a special word which may refer to a special type of reward.
a. True
b. False

66. When we complete the afflictions of Christ, this means:
a. His payment for atonement on the cross was only a down-payment, and was not adequate; we must finish the payment
b. We complete His sufferings as part of His body today, but the atonement was complete, and we do nothing to atone for sins
c. Both are correct
d. Neither is correct

67. As Paul faced his martyrdom in 2 Timothy, we find some truths in that book are:
a. We must seek the best for those who harm us
b. God has given us not a spirit of fear but of self-control
c. God will give us greater power than the suffering we must endure
d. All the above are true
e. a & b are true, but c is false
f. a & c are true, but b is false
g. b & c are true, but a is false

68. What is true?
a. False teachers change the message to avoid suffering

      b.   God protects true teachers so that they do not suffer

      c.   Both are true

      d.   Neither is true

69.   How does God view suffering, and the world view suffering?

      a.   The world considers suffering a tragedy

      b.   God considers suffering for sin a tragedy

      c.   God considers suffering for doing right a tragedy

      d.   All the above are true

      e.   a & b are true, but c is false

      f.   a & c are true, but b is false

      g.   b & c are true, but a is false

70.   What are some marks that we are in Christ's school?

      a.   Persecution

      b.   Suffering

      c.   Martyrdom

      d.   All of the above are true

      e.   a & b are true, but c is false

      f.   a & c are true, but b is false

      g.   b & c are true, but a is false

71.   When we fail, it is usually due to:

      a.   Outside trials

      b.   Inward temptations

72.   Peter writes that we must:

      a.   Trust the Lord in trials

      b.   Live as peaceably as possible

      c.   Be fearful

      d.   Avoid retaliation

      e.   All of the above are true

      f.   All of the above except c are true

      g.   c & d are true, but a & b are false

73.   When fiery trials meet us:

      a.   We must be surprised

      b.   Suffering for good is evidence that God's spirit is on us

c. We must be humble and rest in God's grace

d. We can rejoice knowing that rewards always occur here on earth

e. All of the above are true

f. b & c are true, but a & d are false

g. a, b & c are true, but d is false

74. God promises to:

a. Establish us, giving us a firm foundation

b. Enable us to resist temptation

c. Resist Satan as long as we know that we will not die

d. Restore what is broken down

e. All of the above are true

f. All of the above except b are true

g. All of the above except c are true

75. In Revelation, we find the following about suffering:

a. The Lamb is ultimately victorious, but is slain in battle

b. His messengers overcome, but through suffering and death

c. Testimony involves suffering and death, and Jesus is the faithful witness

d. All the above are true

e. a & c are true, but b is false

f. a & b are true, but c is false

g. b & c are true, but a is false

76. The method of God's ultimate victory includes:

a. The word of their testimony

b. The blood of Christ

c. Force, which leads to hatred and revolt

d. The cross

e. All the above are true

f. All of the above except c are true

g. c & d are true, but a & b are false

77. What is true about suffering for Christ?

a. Satan desires to defeat God's messengers through suffering

    b.   By causing suffering, Satan is able to ultimately thwart God's plans

    c.   God uses suffering for purification

    d.   God uses suffering for discipline

    e.   All of the above are true

    f.   All of the above except b are true

    g.   a & b are true, but c & d are false

78.   What is true about suffering?

    a.   Suffering is always for sin

    b.   Suffering weans us from self-dependence

    c.   Suffering magnifies Christ and His worth

    d.   Suffering magnifies Christ and His grace

    e.   All of the above are true

    f.   All the above except a are true

    g.   All the above except b are true

79.   What is true?

    a.   Suffering is a gift from Jesus Christ, who chose to suffer Himself

    b.   A sacrificial lifestyle makes sense even if there is no life after death

    c.   Jesus Christ chose to suffer; it did not just come upon Him

    d.   All of the above are true

    e.   a & b are true, but c is false

    f.   a & c are true, but b is false

    g.   b & c are true, but a is false

80.   God sometimes uses the enemies of the gospel to multiply churches through persecution and suffering of believers.

    a.   True

    b.   False

81.   What can suffering do for us personally?

    a.   It purifies our motives

    b.   It demonstrates our priorities

    c.   It draws us closer to Christ

    d.   It prepares us for our inheritance in heaven

  e. All of the above
  f. b & c are true, but a & d are false
  g. a & d are true, but b and c are false

82. Suffering can bring:
  a. Glory in heaven
  b. Comfort for ourselves and others
  c. Souls saved as others receive Christ
  d. All of the above are true
  e. a & b are true, but c is false
  f. a & c are true, but b is false
  g. b & c are true, but a is false

ENDNOTES

[1] Barrett, David B. and Johnson, Todd M. "Annual Statistical Table on Global Mission: 2001; International Bulletin of Missionary Research, Vol. 27, No 1, Jan 2003, p. 22

[2] Penner, *op. cit.*, p. 17

[3] Penner, *op. cit.*, p. 7 (preface)

[4] Bonhoeffer, Dietrich, The Cost of Discipleship, Touchdown edition, 1995

[5] http://www.leaderu.com/orgs/probe/docs/bonhoeffer.html

[6] Ton, *op. cit.* pp. 421-436

[7] Penner, *op. cit.* pp. 41-42

[8] 2 Maccabees 7:1-40

[9] The National Christian Evangelical Alliance of Sri Lanka gives several principles to avoid unnecessary provocation in a church situation as a persecuted minority. Be sensitive to the sound level during meetings. Be integrated to the village without alienating the community. Be culturally sensitive to the community around you. Avoid high-publicity programs on special religious holidays. Use relief and social programs as opportunities for relationship but not as bait for evangelism. Adopt a simple lifestyle compatible with the village. Develop unity between Christian leaders. Gather in small communities if hostility is present. Avoid promotion of foreigners and outsiders to prominent positions in the village. Avoid disrespectful comments about other religious groups at all times (Quoted in Penner, *op. cit.* pp 120-121)

[10] Penner, *op. cit.* p 134

[11] Bonhoeffer, D. *The Cost of Discipleship*, p. 242

[12] Ton, *op. cit.*, p. 90

[13] Ton, *op. cit.*, p. 98 ff.

[14] Penner, *op. cit.*, p. 152

[15] Ton, *op.cit.*, p. 86, 104

[16] Ton, *op. cit.*, p. 315

[17] Ton, *op. cit.*, p. 120ff.

18. http://loymershimer.blogspot.com/2005/09/amy-carmichael-have-you-no-scar.html
19. Ignatius: *To Polycarp* p. 3 (Walsh)
20. van Braght, Thieleman J. *Martyr's Mirror*, Herald Press, 1938, p. 108-109
21. van Braght, T., *op. cit.*, pp. 98-99
22. Ton, *op. cit.*, p. 329ff.
23. http://en.wikipedia.org/wiki/Blandina
24. Ton, *op. cit.*, p. 367
25. Foxe's Book of Martyrs, Kindle edition
26. Ton, *op.cit.*, p. 391
27. Two classic books, *Foxe's Book of Martyrs* and *Martyr's Mirror*, outline many of the horrors of this time.
28. Foxe, *op cit.*, p. 57 ff.
29. Wurmbrand, Richard, *In the Face of Surrender*, Bridge Logos Publishers, 1998. This book contains over 200 stories of those persecuted for their faith, primarily in Communist lands. Wurmbrand himself spent 14 years in Romanian prisons undergoing persecution, and 3 years in solitary confinement without speaking to anyone 30 feet below the surface of the ground.
30. Ton, *op. cit.* p. 421 ff.
31. Marshall, Paul, *Their Blood Cries Out*, Word Publishing, Dallas, 1997, 335pp.

INDEX

ABOUT THE AUTHOR

Dr. Robert Patton was born on February 1, 1938 in Cambridge, New York. At age three, he accompanied his parents as missionaries to China. They were moved to the Philippine Islands and spend over three years as Japanese prisoners of war. After returning to the USA, he completed a B.A. at Hamilton College, during which he was a junior Phi Beta Kappa. He married M. Elizabeth Stringham in 1959 and completed his medical degree and was a member of AOA honor society at the University of Rochester School of Medicine. He completed four years of internship and residency in Internal Medicine, followed by two years in the Public Health Service and two years as a cardiology fellow. During this time, he became a specialist and then a fellow in Internal Medicine (FACP). At age 33, Dr. Patton went under the US Public Health Service to Monrovia, Liberia, where he was Professor and Chairman of the Department of Internal Medicine. He was decorated by the Liberian government for his contributions developing this medical program. During these years he was co-author of over 40 scientific papers and co-author of a book on Cardiac Arrythmic Agents. He also accepted the Lord Jesus as savior at age 36 while in Liberia.

The Pattons returned to the USA where he became very active in Grace Baptist Church of South Bend, Indiana while maintaining an internal medical practice with Southwestern Medical Clinic. During these ten years, he completed correspondence studies from Moody Bible Institute and Liberty Home Bible Institute, as well as additional training in counseling. They were called to Suriname, South America, arriving in 1986. During his first five years, Dr. Patton studied Dutch and Sranantongo, opened his first church, and taught in the medical school five mornings a week. He then resigned from medical practice, and concentrated on church planting, translation, and discipleship. He translated the entire Bible with a team between 1991 and 1998, and later wrote commentaries on the entire Bible as well as a number of discipleship studies. He started a Bible Institute in 1991 and an advanced Bible Institute in 2007. The basic Bible Institute is still being run by nationals in 2022. The radio broadcasts which started while the Pattons were in Suriname are continuing on three stations in Paramaribo. For the last four years, they are also being broadcast from radio station Switi Boskopoe by his son-in-law in Moengo, Suriname. They plan for further broadcasts into the interior of Suriname in the near future. The two television programs continue to be broadcast in 2022. Dr. Patton was awarded a Doctor of Divinity from Baptist College of America in 1997.

Dr. Patton and his wife relocated at Crown College in Powell, Tennessee in 2012 while remaining as missionaries under Baptist World Mission. He earned a Master of Ministry in 2013 and a Master of Biblical studies in 2018 from Crown College, and a second Doctor of Divinity from Crown College in 2021.

The Pattons have four children, eighteen grandchildren, and sixteen great-grandchildren. Their son is a missionary in Hungary for nearly 30 years. They have four children with two married. Their son Ben and his wife and baby are missionaries in Zanzibar. Their youngest daughter Kim and her husband are missionaries in Suriname for 33 years with nine children. Four are still in Suriname, and their third son Silas is applying to be a missionary working with them. Their oldest daughter Abigail and her husband and three children are missionaries headed to South Africa. The Pattons older two daughters and their families are serving the Lord in the USA.

QUESTIONS FOR PERSECUTION

OTHER WORKS BY Dr. PATTON

Issues in Missiology Volume 1B Money Matters
Issues in Missiology Volume II
Issues in Missiology Volume III
Issues in Missiology Volume IV (New Edition)
Issues in Missiology Volume V (New Edition)
Marki Foe Wan Disciple
Basis Foe Bribi
Kenki foe Gersi Jezus Kristus
Owroe Testamenti Commentaar Volunes. I, II, III, and IV
Njoe Testamenti Commentaar
Libi Doro da Woortoe
Fondamenti foe Bribi
Broko Dem Boeje

SCIENTIFIC BOOK:

Antiarrhythmic agents: **Arthur** J. **Moss**, M.D., and **Robert D. Patton**, M.D., Springfield, Ill., 1973, Charles C Thomas, Publisher, 161 pp.

193

www.ingramcontent.com/pod-product-compliance
Lightning Source LLC
Chambersburg PA
CBHW060656100426
42734CB00047B/1913